C000046922

Yana Womack

Guardians of the Gate

An Investigation of Numinous Presence, 'Visions of the Divine,' in Dreams

LAP LAMBERT Academic Publishing

Imprint
Any brand names and product names mentioned in this book are subject to trademark, brand or patent protection and are trademarks or registered trademarks of their respective holders. The use of brand names, product names, common names, trade names, product descriptions etc. even without a particular marking in this work is in no way to be construed to mean that such names may be regarded as unrestricted in respect of trademark and brand protection legislation and could thus be used by anyone.

Cover image: www.ingimage.com

Publisher:
LAP LAMBERT Academic Publishing
is a trademark of
International Book Market Service Ltd., member of OmniScriptum Publishing Group
17 Meldrum Street, Beau Bassin 71504, Mauritius

Printed at: see last page
ISBN: 978-3-8383-0498-4

Copyright © Yana Womack
Copyright © 2009 International Book Market Service Ltd., member of OmniScriptum Publishing Group
All rights reserved. Beau Bassin 2009

DEDICATION

in memory of
Anica Vesel Mander

ACKNOWLEDGEMENTS

I would like to thank David Singer for introducing me to the life of dreams, for his guidance, patience and support during all processes of research and writing of this book. I also wish to lovingly acknowledge my longtime mentor, the late Dr. Ani Mander, in appreciation of the many years of friendship we shared and for her constant encouragement of my work. Christopher Castle, artist and specialist in the ways of the numinous inspired me by sharing textures of experience beyond my wildest imaginings. I would especially like to thank the people who generously offered their expertise to this investigation: Dr. Lucia Birnbaum, Steven Halpern, Sven Doehner, Silvia Nakkach, Zakharova Vera Nikolaevna, Batyukova Natalia Ivanovna, Kozlova Zinaida, and Gudkova Tatyana Ivanovna. The field trip to Russia was made possible due to the tireless support and gracious hospitality of Slava Platonov; travels to Nepal were facilitated with the assistance of Basant Bajracharya, Ranju Sharma and Rajendra Shrestha. Deep gratitude goes Tenzin Wangyal Rinpoche for his teachings, and Kusali Devi of Kathmandu and the *kumari* of Bhaktapur for their blessings.

TABLE OF CONTENTS

PROLOGUE: RITUAL AT THE GATE, PURIFICATION AND INVOCATION

May 1st, also referred to as May Day or Beltane,[1] marks the midpoint between the spring equinox and the summer solstice. It is considered the 'fruiting' of the spring. On this fortuitous day, I begin to consolidate all the notes, dream journals and research materials that will coalesce into the writing of this work on my experiences with numinous presence in dreams.

It is an auspicious time for new beginnings. During this year's rite of spring, both the sun and new moon are in the sign of Taurus, ruled by Venus, equated with beauty, peace and harmony. An astrological prognostication reveals it is a pivotal time for creativity "enhanced through embodied relationship with beauty, art and aesthetics. Intentions infused with ideals nourish aspirations from root to flower."[2] It is a favorable period for devoting full attention to the numinous "guardians of the gates," the figures and forces that have visited me in the imaginal landscapes of my dreams for over a decade.

This midpoint day marks the ripest day of spring, a time that was traditionally celebrated in Maypole dances, fire-jumping festivals, play, love-making, dressing in green clothing and collecting hawthorn blossoms (mayflowers)[3] for wreaths to crown the maypole. A Druid's calendar pronounces,

> Drink from a well before sunrise. Wash in the morning dew, and adorn yourselves with greenery. . . watch the sun come up, dance 'round the Maypole, and otherwise abandon yourself to the season. A woodland frolic culminating in indiscretion is the order of the day.[4]

It was believed the dew gathered before sunrise on the eve of May Day contained a beautifying essence imbued with healing powers, a magical elixir of the earth.[5] In Lithuania, my maternal homeland, this precious dew was referred to as *rasa*.[6]

On May Day eve, I set the intention to wake up at four in the morning, before sunrise, so I can anoint myself with the morning dew. I awake naturally at 3:55 A.M. and walk to the backyard to a patch of clover. I cup the dew in my hands, sprinkle my face and body and proceed to anoint my entire being. I collect a small amount in a glass and return to the house to consecrate my Tara[7] statue at her altar, a couple drops for the bronze dakini and winged snake deity from Nepal, and with the few remaining drops I sprinkle over my partner David in the next room who lay there fast asleep. Being present during this liminal time, I enter into a relationship with the turning of the year. I participate by situating myself at the apex of the thin boundaries, the precipice of a time / space continuum where guardians of the gates reside, a time during the year when fairies are believed to dance in the borderlands and dakinis are known to whisper in one's ear.

This early hour, so serene, also marks the threshold between dark and light, night and day, my dreaming and waking time. The corridor between May Day until the summer solstice is said to be a time of increase and abundance. I stand before the new moon to receive her blessings. In days to come, I will watch her horned crescent form in the night sky—a reminder she is near.[8]

In mid-morning I carry the statue of the female buddha Green Tara out to the middle of the patch of clover, still glistening with dew. First I wrap her in my finest white linen ritual cloth, walk over to the rose bushes and pick the whitest and reddest rose (to represent purity, passion) while silently reciting the Tara mantra, "Om Tare Tuttare Ture Svha." Then, I lay her softly down in the bed of clover, carefully placing the white and red rose petals on and all around her. She lay there on the earth adorned in flowers, facing the twilight sky. She appears as a spirit of nature in the lush green grass and clover.

"The Plant Medicine Sutra" by Robert Schrei in *Zig Zag Zen* comes to mind,

Thus I have heard. That night the bodhisattva awoke and found herself surrounded by vines, branches, flowers, roots, sap, essence of the plant world, and the wildness of nature, all supplicating her for a teaching that would illumine their minds. The bodhisattva spoke: No, it is you, not I, who needs to speak; it is you, it is your

2

voice that is needed to awaken the self-centered human species to the vast web of life and love and awareness that is the intimate birthright of us all.[9]

A crow flies overhead. Curious to know what the crow signifies, I later turn to my books on symbolism. Ted Andrews states,

> Wherever crows are, there is magic. They are symbols of creation and spiritual strength. They remind us to look for opportunities to create and manifest the magic of life. Crows are messengers calling to us about the creation and magic that is alive within our world everyday and available to us.[10]

Next, I look up the word crow in the *Dictionary of Symbols* by J.E. Cirlot, "Because of its black colour, the crow is associated with the idea of beginnings (as expressed in such symbols as the maternal night, primigenial darkness, the fertilizing earth)."[11] In medieval times, black used to represent the *nigredo*, "the initial state of substance—unformed but full of potential."[12] It is also connected to divination, mystical powers and is believed to be a messenger of prophetic powers. "Its caw played a special part in rites of divination."[13] In Poland (my paternal homeland), the crow is considered an epiphany of the *czarownica* (one who enchants) in her role as the shapeshifting crone.

Later in the day, I place Tara back on her pedestal in my study. At the base of the statue, I place a flesh-colored stone that is in the shape of a tongue. It is a gift from a Nepalese friend who leads pilgrimages to Mount Kailash. The stone is from *Drolma La*, Tibetan for "Tara Pass," situated 18,000 feet high in the northernmost region of the Himalayas and is considered a very sacred place on this most holy mountain.[14] It is believed that if one is able to cross the pass, it is likened to rebirth. Tara's epitaph is "she who helps cross over." I place the stone infused with her essence in front of the Tara statue and humbly request her assistance. I ask Tara to guide me in the months ahead, to grant me permission to speak of my sacred dreams so that others may benefit from this path of inquiry,[15] and to lift the veil of the boundary spaces so the other-worldly presences and forces can speak to me and through me, provide me with blessings, clarity and insight during the writing of this book.

I think of the numerical significance of the day 5-1-03 that when added up equals nine, a number associated with the triple goddess,[16] another auspicious indication of this special day. Up to this point, this project has been incubating, gestating, churning, shifting, forming and developing. Now, the "prima materia," gathered in a large white notebook (an illustration of a mirror-imaged guardian of the gate at each side of a spinning ouroboros adorning its cover) is ready for manifestation.

Reflecting on the concept of *rasa*,[17] I begin to recognize a perspective I adopted since I was a pre-teen—framing beauty—to appreciate the sacred or essence in things, the rasa of the moment, to take in the aesthetic experience that is offered all around us and open to the numinous. It is more a working with the light, instead of the dark, a practice I feel is fundamental for the gentle cultivation of sensitivity to subtle signs and messages that occur in waking life and in dreams.

CHAPTER 1: INTRODUCTION, ENTERING THE GATE

Personal Introduction

As a child growing up in the Berkshires in New England, I was enchanted by the many cultural offerings available including: art shows, classical music concerts, dance recitals and summer stock theater. I found the greatest pleasure in imagining the worlds and stories that seemed to peak through the imagery hanging on the walls in the art galleries. The graceful, precise movements of the costumed dancers, the convincing embodiment of characters by the actors on stage, and the music of Chopin or Bach filled my childhood and early adult inner world with a brilliant and rich vitality. I was also fascinated with the way artists, musicians, actors and dancers viewed the world. They used a language that did not entirely rely on words, but drew from a vocabulary of images and symbols, sounds, movement, shade and color as their mediums of creating expressions of the numinous into being.

The impetus for this work on numinous presence in dreams is derived in part from my first memory—being a magic fairy.

I am three years old running / flying clockwise around the outside of our newly built white house that borders a farmer's field and forest. Next door in a fenced pasture two cows lazily graze. On this summer day, the landscape glows emerald green, the sun warms and glistens my skin, and the air is infused with the smell of mowed grass. I am a gossamer-winged fairy waving my sparkling magic wand as I fly. I am filled with complete and utter joy. As I recognize this full, ecstatic, blissful feeling, I make note to myself then and there to always remember this moment. Then, I proceed to fly, then land with a big splash into the blue vinyl swimming pool.

Thinking back on this memory I can still recall my firm commitment to remember it; it seemed so real and significant. I never wanted to forget it. Now, decades later, I find this memory remains as one of my most gifted treasures. It recaptures the essence of my childhood innocence, joy, sense of wonder and curiosity. It initiated a world view that places value on the moment, the aesthetic, authentic, mystical, and transformative experience. This experience gave birth to the observation that if I turn my attention to what exists beyond ordinary consciousness and enter into the realms of the imaginal where displays of the numinous occur, I am afforded access to a wider field of vision. Life's abundant riches—gifts of wondrous beauty, spaciousness, teachings, and connections—are always available. It's a matter of *seeing, being.*

Over the years I have been reminded (through meditation practices, contemplation and study) that participating in the realms of the numinous is a matter of letting go, being in the moment and opening to the visual displays, the sounds, expressions of the transcendent and numinous, yet not getting attached to them. Adopting this viewpoint has taught me about freeing the imagination and a belief in possibilities that extend beyond the limits of human cognition. I discovered that yielding to life's gifted moments requires an attitude of trust, somatic awareness, maintaining a fresh outlook ('beginner's mind')[18] being with love, empathy and compassion, paying attention and ultimately understanding the difference between 'essence' and personality.[19]

The theme of the magical fairy or skywoman continued to develop over the course of my life which led to in-depth investigations into women and mythology, religion, folklore, shamanism, and women's roles as healers in pre-Christian Europe. I participation in Buddhist meditation practices to Tara and the dakini and researched imagery, ritual objects, amulets, and adornments associated with "skydancers" (*dakinis*), yoginis, female deities, shamans, the *rusalki, baba,* and other women of power and wisdom. Further work on the "space-going woman" or skydancer was inspired by fieldwork conducted in India (Calcutta, Bhubaneswar, and Puri) and Nepal (Kathmandu Valley and Pokhara) in 1998, and again in 2000. Since then, I have continued to lead pilgrimages to the Kathmandu Valley in particular to the Mother Goddess Durga Festival, *Dasain.*[20]

I found manifestations of the numinous abundantly evident in the East. There was life at its most vital; nothing remained behind closed doors. It was life unmasked. In Nepal, I was surrounded by a cadence of sights, sounds, tastes related to the domain of

6

the spiritual (vibrant red hibiscus and marigold flowers on shrines—offerings to Durga, monks in burgundy and saffron robes circumambulating the stupa at Boudhanath reciting the mantra *Om Mani Padme Hum*, the dreadlocked ascetic sadhus with marks symbolizing Shiva worship on their foreheads, the smell of cardamom chai brewing, women dressed in colorful, diaphanous saris, and wafting juniper incense intoxicating me as I strolled the unpaved roads of Pashupatinath, where in the distance smoke rose from the burning ghats, evidence of a ritual to the deceased.

Living in the United States, I miss this palatable aliveness and pervasive atmosphere of the divine. Perhaps it is in part why I avidly maintain practices that connect me to the sacred unseen realms. In *The Spell of the Sensuous,* David Abram articulates his reaction to the heady vibrancy of the East and compares it to living in the United States.

> I began to see and to hear in a manner I never had before. . . my ears began to attend, in a new way, to the songs of birds no longer just a melodic background to human speech, but meaningful speech in its own right, responding to and commenting on events in the surrounding earth. I became a student of subtle differences . . . walking along the dirt paths, I learned to slow my pace in order to feel the difference between one nearby hill and the next, or to taste the essence of a particular field at a certain time of day . . . There the air was a thick and richly textured presence, filled with invisible but nonetheless tactile, olfactory, and audible influences. In the United States, however, the air seemed thin and void of substance or influence. It was not, here, a sensuous medium—the felt matrix of our breath and the breath of the other animals and plants and soils—but was merely an absence, and indeed was constantly referred to in everyday discourse as mere empty space . . . What was it that made possible the heightened sensitivity to extra human reality, the profound attentiveness to other species and to the Earth that is evidenced in so many of these cultures, and that had so altered my awareness that my senses now felt stifled and starved by the patterns of my own culture?. . . How had Western civilization come to be so exempt from this sensory reciprocity . . . so deaf and blind of the vital existence of other species, and to the animate landscapes they inhabit, that we now so casually bring about their destruction?[21]

Numinous practices sustain and enliven me. They remind me to recognize and value the sacred in my daily experiences. Now, instead of imagining to be the magic fairy, as recalled from childhood, I engage in transformative embodiment practices of the Tibetan Buddhist and ancient Bon spiritual traditions. In Guru Yoga,[22] I meditate envisioning myself as Tara, the *dakini,*[23] or *Taparitza.*[24] In dreams, I interact with lions, deer, snakes, flowers, and ocean waves. I fly above the clouds or travel to places inside the earth to receive counsel and healing from my animal allies in shamanic journeys and commune with eggs, various shapes, lights, forms and forces of nature in Authentic Movement and Holotropic Breathwork. For renewal, I regularly pilgrimage to sacred sites in the East in order to meld and re-engage with the numinous in atmospheres reinforced and supported by the culture.

Driven by a need to explore my roots, I traveled to Eastern Europe (Russia) in 2002. I had the opportunity to join an ethnographic expedition with Mary B. Kelly,[25] author Sheila Paine,[26] Slava Platonov, and Valentina Elam to study the folk costumes and rituals of the Volga peoples during a Midsummer's Festival in Cheboksary, Russia, land of the Chuvash, a people claimed to be linked to the ancient Amazons.[27] As a sub-study, I researched Slavic and Chuvash supernatural symbolism in the embroidered motifs and horned headdresses in women's folk dress, and the Baba Yaga figure, the *matrioshka,* and *rusalki* of the Slavic folk traditions. In Cheboksary I met with local folklore experts and museum curators, conducted interviews on the topic of women's folk practices, and received counsel and healing treatments from a female doctor trained in both allopathic and Siberian shamanic medicine. In Chapter 6, I draw from travel notes about this journey that relates to my Personal Mythology dreams.

Always amazed at the unerring, abundant love bestowed upon me in my dreams, my heart overflows with gratitude. Now, I feel the need to reciprocate. Rarely have I taken the time to properly acknowledge the numinous presences, meet them, see them, and engage with them in my waking life. Although I wrote the dreams down so not to forget the main characters and themes, I rarely stopped to examine them thoroughly. This work is an endeavor to give them my full undivided attention, to embrace and honor the numena of the liminal dream spaces.

In the fall of 1992, I began to document my dreams. In the summer of the same year, I met collage artist and symbolist, David Singer (well-known for his counterculture Fillmore rock posters of the 1970's). Often, we would stay up into the early morning hours discussing ancient spiritual practices, perusing images (he has an enormous collection of images for his work), and examining iconography of Egyptian stelae, and ancient Pre-Columbian artifacts with large magnifiers. David would read me passages from his impressive library of anthropology, religion, folklore, and mythology, pointing out etymological associations and other connections. I became riveted to this new way of seeing. Newly absorbed in ancient symbolism related to the sacred woman for the jewelry business I had recently established, I was enthusiastic to learn more. David affirmed that a craft can be a gateway into wells of the numinous realms. I began to look within at an inner dimension beginning to unfold through rumblings of evocative dreams that would mark the beginning of a transformational period that would last for well over a decade.

It was not only the imagery and the new connections that I was discovering, and the dreams that contributed to my growing interest in the mysterious workings of the unseen worlds, but the actual relationship with David that I believe provided the foundation for the surge of the consciousness expansion I was beginning to notice. I felt truly seen, heard, honored, and nurtured. I was able to relax into myself, held by his unconditional, spacious love. David called me "Yana," a name my Polish grandmother used to affectionately call me when I was a girl. (My birth name is Jane which is Yana in Polish). Yana means 'the path' or 'vehicle' in Sanskrit. In time, the significance of this name would reveal to me threads to an ancient past and a gateway to a personal mythology.

My dreams began to mirror my metamorphosis. Early on, I had a dream that I was born from a pulsating fetus-like egg. I began to observe a parallel life beginning to take form. From an infant growing up among protective animals, to a girl, then woman who all along received nurturance, guidance, and protection from numinous dream figures, I

9

couldn't help but notice there was a community of sacred beings watching over me, wanting to help me.

Being the eldest child, I became used to the position of guide and protector, a kind of second mother in command. In a previous marriage and in other relationships, I often took on a co-dependent role, concentrating more on my partner's successes and advancements instead of my own. Now, it was my turn to be nurtured. As I began to surrender, drinking in the love and attention so generously offered from the dream numena and in waking life, everything appeared fresh and new. Even the air seemed charged.

Just previous to the onset of the numinous dream series, I had experienced a major life crisis. Chronic tension from working in a corporate environment for close to a decade, tracing courier packages for irrate customers under the constant scrutiny of demanding managers, commuting hours in heavy traffic, etc., subsequently impregnated me with a uterine fibroid tumor the size of a small grapefruit, a non-entity that was nourished with coffee, wine, cigarettes and tranquilizers, sucking up my life force like a vacuum. This medical issue signaled that I needed to pay attention to my health and cease putting energy into a unproductive, unhealthy lifestyle. I deserved more. I carried around so much tension that one day I knew I had to quit my job. As I sat there in the rest room frozen in a panic attack, my heart audibly pounding, wondering how I was going to flee without being seen, I felt as if I was falling apart, in pieces, yet at the same time as if I was disappearing.

After surgical removal of the tumor and quitting the job, I attended to my health and psyche. Through a regimented healing program of massage, diet, yoga, spiritual guidance and a regular meditation practice,[28] I began a pilgrimage of recovery.[29] My dream guides responded to me with open arms (and wings). I moved in with David and began to gestate, then enter, through the numinous gates to a fresh new panorama of a renewed Yana emerging.

Everyone dreams. Some of us don't remember our dreams at all. Others remember remnants of them that fade by the time we finish our morning coffee. Then, there are some who have epic dreams[30] containing intricate, complex layers and cryptic messages. There are people who wake up frightened by nightmares, and dreamers who arise in a hazy light of heavenly bliss from visits to worlds "where people fly and water runs uphill."[31]

For many cultures throughout the world, dreaming is considered as real as waking. Dreams have been known to provide not only healing but spiritual connection, guidance, and insight. An integration of them into daily waking life is considered healthy for the individual and for the community. Dreams have also inspired great works of art and other creative endeavors, discoveries of healing methods, and religions.[32]

The numinous dreams I have collected over the past decade can be categorized as healing, ecstatic, mystical, transcendent, initiatory, visionary, and lucid. Most have a spiritual message or theme. This is not to say *all* my dreams are characteristic of the numinous, are lucid, and that I remember them all the time. Sometimes I go months without remembering any. The ones I have written down, however, are my special dreams where familiar characters have revisited and patterns emerged. They are the dreams where I am given gifts, initiations, transmissions, guidance, prophecy, consolation, loving protection, and healings.

Numinous Presence

Numinous means 1) "of, or pertaining to a *numen*," 2) "divine, spiritual, revealing or suggesting the presence of a god," and, 3) "inspiring awe and reverence." Numen (*numena*, pl.) is described as a "deity, divinity, divine or presiding power, or spirit."[33] It is also referred to as a *daimon*, hierophant, genius, angel, among other appellations. As a "perceivable manifestation, it is psychologically and viscerally experienced as a presence, the manifestation of something specifically sensed by the psyche."[34]

An intention of this work is to contribute to the corpus of primary experiences in dream study from the perspective of an American woman in midlife. It is an investigation of self-discovery drawn from selected dreams recorded in journals for over a decade (between the years 1992 to 2003). Specifically I focus on dreams that have inspired my spiritual path—meetings with numinous wisdom guides. In these dreams, the poetic and metaphoric landscapes of the imaginal are conveyed to me in words, images, intuitions, transmissions and through the channeling and the senses. Examination of these dreams has facilitated a growing understanding of the supra-subtle ripenings of the unseen realms.

An integral methodology—a combination of modified Heuristic Research Methods[35] and Organic Inquiry[36] serves to support the imaginal, transformative, and autobiographical aspects and the *living* qualities of this investigation.

The study unfolds in a three-fold process. First, in the Immersion Phase, I identify the numena that will be included in the investigation. Next, in the Amplification Phase, I meet the numena through the techniques involving the discovery of personal, symbolic and mythic connections.[37] In the Engagement Phase, I creatively interact with them. I draw on Daniel Deslaurier's postulate that dream work, the sense of conscious engagement with dream contents before, during or after dreaming leads one to a fuller engagement with the self and the spirit, as well as nurtures the "mature unfolding of spiritual and emotional intelligence."[38]

By opening to both the presence of the numinous dream figures and their guidance illuminates and influences my "root metaphors"[39] and soul's purpose. Mythic and waking stories co-emerge, one informing the other, allowing for synchronicities, cues, symbols, images, and concepts to take on a deeper, fuller significance.[40] Themes that arise from this process offer clearer insights into connections not previously considered.

Spiritually Transformative Dreams

While researching the classifications of dreams, I discovered various categories including: ordinary dreams, healing dreams,[41] lucid dreams,[42] waking dreams,[43] recurring dreams,[44] spiritual dreams,[45] and others. I was fortunate to come across a new pioneering work by Stanley Krippner, Fariba Bogzaran, and Andre Percia De Carvalho, *Extraordinary Dreams and How to Work with Them*. It addressed the type of dreams I experience. I also drew inspiration from the work of Rhea White—"Extraordinary Human Experiences,"[46] and Yvonne Kason's study on "Spiritually Transformative Experiences" in which she describes spiritual experiences in spontaneous lucid dreams and mystical states, as well as discusses the understanding that dreams provide guidance and insight to further one's spiritual path.[47]

Thus, in line with Kason's definition of the Spiritually Transformative Experience, I categorize the numinous dreams in this study as *Spiritually Transformative Dreams*. The first category of dreams, *Clarity dreams* is inspired by the Buddhist Nyingma school and Bon traditions of Tibet and is primarily grounded in the work of Tenzin Wangyal Rinpoche, Namkhai Norbu, and Serinity Young. The second category is classified as *Initiation dreams,* and the third category, *Personal Mythology* (dreams that inform one's personal core life theme)—both drawn from the work of Stanley Krippner, Fariba Bogzaran, and Andre Percia de Carvalho.[48]

Clarity dreams

Tenzin Wangyal Rinpoche in *The Tibetan Yogas of Dream and Sleep* defines a Clarity dream in relation to the shamanic worldview of the ancient Bon tradition of Tibet. Rinpoche states,

> The clarity dream is beyond an ordinary dream of increased awareness. It arises when the mind and the prana are balanced and the dreamer has developed the capacity to remain in non-personal presence . . . The dream of clarity includes more objective knowledge, which arises from collective karmic traces and is

13

available to consciousness when it is not entangled in personal karmic traces . . . the consciousness is then not bound by space and time and personal history, and the dreamer can meet with real beings, receive teachings from real teachers, and find information helpful to others as well as to him or herself.[49]

Clarity dreams may arise spontaneously or result from meditation practice—training the mind to be still.[50] In the introduction to *Dream Yoga* by Namkhai Norbu, Michael Katz explains, The Clarity dream "seem[s] to arise out of intense mental concentration upon a particular problem or subject, as well as through meditation and ritual."[51] It is not uncommon for them to manifest during meditation retreats.

Clarity dreams may be incubated. Dream incubation has been practiced for millennia. Healing sanctuaries situated on geomantic sites often near springs were the settings of requested dreams. Physical, mental, emotional and psychic healings are often the result of incubated Clarity dreams. Even a single Clarity dream in one's life is shown to have profound effects. It is a way to connect with the spirit and unseen forces often inspiring epiphanies leading to great discoveries, and innovative creative expressions.

Visionary aspects (oracular, supernatural, precognitive and / or psychic) include: finding oneself channeling or being channeled images,[52] words, sounds; precognitions or receiving visions of future events; seeing underlying causes of situations; and understanding subtle, non-verbal communications.

Clarity dreams are similar to lucid dreams[53] in the sense that one is aware that she or he is dreaming and is thus able to change the course of the dream, or recall a dream within a dream, but different in that qualities of clarity are situated within a spiritual orientation. These dreams may be classified in the same category as mystical visions in Spiritually Transformative Experiences.[54] Sometimes called "big dreams," or holy dreams, they are characterized as having transpersonal or mystical qualities.

Episodes of ecstatic experiences, heightened sensual and emotional qualities, and intermodal *syntheasia*,[55] a synthesis of all senses combined, are pronounced characteristics of Clarity dreams. Feelings of unbounded freedom, mergings, *darsan*,[56]

14

experiences of *samadhi*, elevation and transcendence may occur. Clarity dreams foster a clarity of awareness, a conscious luminosity that often bridges into waking life. Hence, recognition of them is beneficial for one's spiritual path as it provides a felt connection to the sublime.

It has been found these dreams most often occur in early mornings, from a lighter sleep when the mind is calm and stable. Upon awakening, one may feel in a state of awe, or as if one has been bestowed with grace. Often this is accompanied with an overwhelming sense of gratitude and love.

There are many types of Clarity dreams. To stay within the scope of this inquiry, I concentrate on one aspect and investigate dreams that contain the numena of sound. The divine presence of sound is met in Chapter 5 through the contemplation of dreams that feature mantras, the throat chakra, the *rasa* of delight through sound, and a ritualistic meeting with Shiva.

Personal Mythology dreams

Personal Mythology dreams is a term derived from a category of dreams described in Krippner, Bogzaran, and de Carvalho's work on extraordinary dreams. They point out,

> Personal myths are woven from many strands including the events of the past, the mythos of the culture in which the dreamer was raised and lives . . . and those inspirational moments that allow a person to sense the spiritual essence of the universe and peer into its nature . . . Since personal mythology often is rooted in the ways the dreamer learned to make sense of the world during childhood . . . the mythic worldview that develops . . . largely determined by the hopes, fears, strengths, and weaknesses of one's parents and by other circumstances beyond one's control . . . shapes a person's desires, attitudes, and choices just as unconscious psychodynamics shape one's dream life. While personal mythologies continually mature throughout the years and a dreamer may have some consciousness access into that process, it is a realm that operates largely below the level of awareness for most people. [Thus, the examination of personal mythology dreams help the spiritual quester integrate her or his] existing mythic structure with the data of ongoing life experiences.[57]

15

In Chapter 6, I discuss aspects of my journey to the Slavic lands in relation to a dream about a mother doll. The Mother numena is met and contemplated in her roles as wisdom guide, the earth, and grandmother. Meeting the Mother numena, then engaging with the *matrioska* in ritual illuminates a vital, personal, mythic thread to my ancestral roots, as well as provides insights into some East European spiritual and folklore practices.

Initiation dreams

Initiation dreams is a category of dreams borrowed from the work of Krippner, Bogzaran, and de Carvalho. They are defined as dreams of being approached by a deity, spirit or guardian, or numinous teacher for instruction, transmissions or initiations, and / or healings.[58] Krippner, Bogzaran, and de Carvalho further describes these dreams,

> Initiation dreams were accepted as direct contacts with the supernatural entities who affected the destiny of the clan, the tribe, or the community. These deities, spirits, or guardians could instruct the dreamer in the lore and wisdom of his or her people, ordain him or her as their messenger, and confer various powers, privileges, and duties.[59]

In Chapter 7, I focus on meeting the skywomen. The term "skywoman" pertains to the numen as a woman of wisdom, one who shapeshifts or transcends the boundaries of space and time, i.e., the *jana* or women's spirit guardian, the bird woman, *rusalki*, *dakini*, yogini, and the shaman. My interactions in dreams with her include periods when she, I, or both of us are flying, dancing, spinning, or shapeshifting. A quality of the skywoman is her ability to transform things with her mind, perform magical feats, offer empowerments (initiations so that experiences of expanded capacities of awareness can be experienced). In this chapter, I discuss a dream of a hawk woman, research the skywomen's various epiphanies, then creatively engage with her and other skywomen in ritual.

Although some overlap occurs, i.e., elements of Clarity dreams may be evident in Personal Mythology dreams, etc., in this investigation I attempt to stay within the ranges of the three dream types in order to illustrate how orienting to the predominant themes creates pathways for further illuminations.

Results from the methodology are presented in two sections in Chapter 8. In Part 1: Reflections on Immersion and Amplification, I discuss the Immersion Phase, how I arrived at the topic and organized the research data. Then, I offer findings resulting from the Amplification Phase of the study (meeting the numena through mytho-religious research and personal connections). In Part 2: Yana at the Gate: Reflections on Engaging with Dream Numena, I discuss the Engagement Phase (communing with the numena), and reflections on the rituals.

In Chapter 9, Synthesis, are final words on what I discovered to be the significant highlights of the study—what particularly stood out, revelations, insights, and connections made. Concluding, I provide suggestions for applications of this work in guidance practices, therapeutic counseling and personal development inquiry.

CHAPTER 2: NUMINOUS PRESENCE IN DREAMS, EASTERN AND WESTERN PERSPECTIVES

In this chapter, I present a discussion on the foundational literature of dream researchers in the fields of psychology, mythology, and religion. Also included and specific to this study is documentation related to spiritual transformation and numinous dreams. It furthers conversations in the development of: 1) empathy and compassion—values clearly needed in today's world; 2) personal mythologies that enhance depth of meaning in life, and 3) initiatory rites of passage, particularly at mid-life.

Numen, Numena, Numinous

What is a *numen*? Many have likely heard of the term *numinous* but numen is not a word generally used in everyday language. As mentioned earlier, the term numen (*numena*, pl.) central to this investigation, is defined as a deity, spiritual entity, angel, *daimon*, hierophant, genius, or *jana*.[60] It is sensed by the psyche as a presence. The numen does not always appear as a reified form, however, and may manifest as an invisible force or a presence, i.e., a wave, a sound, a shimmery light, etc.

Numinous is the adjective pertaining to numen, a word coined by Rudolf Otto primarily in reaction to moralistic interpretations of the word holy, i.e., holy man, connoting one's exemplary moral behavior. In his book, *The Idea of the Holy*,[61] Otto argued that an over-intellectual approach to religion undermined the emotional and more non-rational qualities of holiness and the sacred. Thus, he used the more neutral term "numinous" derived from the Latin *numen*, meaning the divine spirit in nature. He felt the term numinous more efficaciously exemplified the heart of the sacred. Otto asserted that "when we speak of God, our words capture ideas or when we think of God, we use concepts to grasp the nature of the Divine." He believed the Holy or Sacred, which he referred to as experiences of non-rational, sublime, and awesome moments eludes comprehension and are ineffable and inexpressible.[62]

Elaborating on the term 'sacred,' Otto coined the words *hierophany*, and *mysterium tremendum*. "Hierophany" refers to the manifestation of the sacred, a revelation of a reality which is entirely different from the mundane. It can be a power or force which is unique from anything we have encountered and can only be experienced. It characterizes the non-intellectual, feeling, and emotional state, the experience of the sensual and the spiritual, or sacred presence of the divine.

"Mysterium tremendum" is a term Otto used to refer to a feeling of awe, fascination or longing. He argued that the numinous only pertained to religious experience and thus could not be demonstrated by argument or theory. "Since Otto's book there has been little discussion in regards to the distinction made between the 'sacred' and the 'holy.'"[63]

Numena as Angelic

Numena can be described as angelic.[64] In *The Physics of Angels,* Matthew Fox and Rupert Sheldrake define "angel" as "a ministering spirit or divine messenger . . . attendants and messengers of the Deity."[65] Sheldrake discusses the angel's shapeshifting abilities in reference to a passage by Hildegard de Bingen, "According to their nature angels are invisible but they take their bodies from the atmosphere and appear visible in human form to those they are sent to as messengers."[66] He posits that "Hildegard is talking about the shapeshifting power of angels, who can manifest in almost any form appropriate to the circumstances. They can speak in human tongues and if necessary, can appear to be human . . . Their embodiment can have a curiously real and literal presence."[67]

Numena as Shapeshifters

As shapeshifters,[68] numena travel beyond the boundaries of space and time, appear out of nowhere, disappear, change shape, size, express themselves through the senses, or by way of "felt presence," etc. There is a particular quality of reversibility and movement that is characteristic of shapeshifters and spirits. They are associated symbolically with the reverse of how humans live with night replacing day, etc. This reversibility is evident in rituals, incantations,[69] and dream maps called *ittals.*[70] Healing spells are in many cases recited backwards, and in rituals, one turns to the left instead of to the right.[71] Not only do numena travel reverse paths but non-linear ones. Recalling the words of Plotinus, James Hillman writes, "The soul moves in circles. Hence our lives are not moving straight ahead; instead, hovering, wavering, returning, renewing, repeating."[72]

Numena as Genius, Daimon

The concept of genius is analogous to the numen. Barbara Walker states that genius (plural *genie*) is a Roman term that referred to guardian spirits for men.

> It was a word for a "spirit of paternal ancestry, cognate with Arabic *djinn*, or *genie*. Each Roman man had his personal *genius* as a guardian angel or familiar; each woman had a corresponding female spirit called a *juno* [before *juno*, a *jana*]. In the time of the empire, the word *genius* came to be applied to both sexes . . . The meaning of genius changed again in the Middle Ages, when it was virtually synonymous with 'spirit.'. . . The modern meaning, an exceptionally intelligent or inspired persona was of late origin.[73]

Ralph Metzner explains the word *daimon* refers to a spirit, later 'demonized.'[74] In *The Unfolding Self,* Metzner asserts,

> Our word *demon* actually comes from the Greek *daimon* which was originally not an evil spirit at all. It was a protective spirit, a divine guardian, something like what later European folklore called the guardian angel . . . It was only under the later influence of Christian dogmatism that the word *demon* came to have maleficent connotations."[75]

Research on Numinous Presence in Dreams

Specific to my topic on numinous presence in dreams, I was able to locate the following investigations that contributed to this work. The results of the search included: 1) "Personal Dreamscape as Personal Landscape," by Karen Jaenke, an inspiring dissertation on a woman's indigenous dreams; 2) "Living on the Edge: Personal Experiences as the New Dispensation in the Age of Aquarius" by Marina Ferrier, a combined heuristic, hermeneutic, and phenomenological study on numinous experiences; 3) "The Experience of the Numinous in the Imaginal Dream Group Process known as DreamTending" by Patricia Ann Sablatura explaining how the dream group provides a container for discussion and strong bonds of connection with oneself and others; and 4) "A Heuristic Investigation of Presence" by Marc Stuckey stating how encounters with numinous entities manifest in those who surrender their egos to the present "lived moment." I found there were few books on Clarity dreams,[76] none specifically on sound dreams, although I was able to locate an interesting article by psychologist, Sven Doehner,[77] "Sound Transformation in Dream-Work: Nourishing the Soul."

Spiritual Intelligence

During the fall of 2000, I attended a lecture by Professor Daniel Deslauriers at California Institute of Integral Studies in San Francisco in which he spoke about "Spiritual intelligence." It was one of those moments when one feels a shift, an epiphany. I had heard of emotional intelligence,[78] but not spiritual intelligence. This concept piqued my interest. It also gave me pause to think if I hadn't thought of it then it probably hadn't occurred to others either. The idea of spiritual intelligence is not valued in our culture like logical intelligence. I sat there considering all the implications of this omission.[79] I attributed it partially to the word 'spiritual'. It may be that people related the concept of spirituality with the dogmas and hegemonies of organized religions.

Reflecting back on Deslauriers' lecture, inspired, I read an essay in which he elaborated on the term. Deslauriers states:

Spiritual intelligence, like intelligence in general, is related to the ability to absorb information, to learn and to cope, to understand and deal with new situations and to the ability to apply knowledge in making choices or in thinking abstractly (essential to the development of dream skills). It is, however, concerned with distinctive dimensions of thinking, being, affect and action that lead to greater authenticity, openness, compassion, truthfulness, moral or ethical concerns, as well as the exploration of ultimate values.[80]

Deslauriers shares with us Roger Lipsey's[81] definition of spiritual. It is similar to sacred in its description of holiness:

[Spiritual] is an incursion from above or deep within to which the ordinary human being can only surrender . . . It needn't be called 'the spiritual' but words of some kind will be found to describe an intelligence, a vitality, a sense of deliverance from pettiness and arrival at dignity that always seems a gift. It includes a perception of grandeur in the world at large which cannot help but strike us as sacred, quite beyond oneself and yet there to be witnessed and even shared in.[82]

Next, I present an overview of prominent voices on the hermeneutics of the numinous dream experience, specifically explaining how dreams were understood in ancient times and how they are viewed today, beginning with Western culture, and then discussing dream practices in the East.

Are Dreams Real?

Are dreams real? In the West, dreams are generally not taken seriously. Westerners have been socialized to ignore and dismiss their dreams although many scientific discoveries have been inspired by numinous dreams. Our inherited Western culture's foundational roots—Christianity and scientific modernism have contributed to the devaluation of what our ancestors once held sacred and have influenced the inhibition of expressions of unseen realms. The reexamination of the Newtonian / Cartesian paradigm in the past couple decades indicates there is a revival of interest in the numinous. It

22

appears there exists a profound need to reconnect with energies that we may not be able to name but which we once shared as a matter of course.

Although dreams are generally not acknowledged, or validated in modern Western culture, evidence for the use of dream incubation for healing and inspiration spans back to Classical Greece and beyond. Greek oracle centers called the *Aesculapia* (such as the *Epidauros*) were visited regularly for healing dreams and for purposes of connecting to one's numena.[83]

Proponents to the theory of the reality of dreams include psychologist Stephen Aizenstat. *DreamTending* is a technique developed by Dr. Aizenstat, who is well known for his work on the psychodynamic process of 'tending the living image' in dreamwork. Aizenstat states that dream figures seem alive like living images.

> They have bodies, they move about; they interact with one another; and they inhabit very specific locations. . . . When practicing DreamTending over time, we find ourselves frequenting these landscapes and encountering these figures time and again and even establishing ongoing 'friendships' with a number of them . . . Living images function as intermediaries between the dreamer and the dreaming psyche. Appearing most often as a particular figure, the living image relates the dreamer to very specific life circumstances—to personal history or to an inner-subjective experience . . . The art of DreamTending offers a portal to the poetics of imagination. In tending dreams, images are vivified, the psyche animated. We become curious and open in the process. We befriend the archetypal imagination, and we are in turn welcomed into the presence of soul.[84]

Krippner, et al share an interesting discovery regarding similar neurological functions in waking and dreaming:[85]

> It makes sense to consider that dreams are just as 'real' as waking experience, a position held thousands of years ago by tribal shamans. The neural patterns that are activated while a person is awake are similar to those activated while that person is asleep. What an individual perceives is thus of equal substance and equally 'real' in both states of consciousness. We see this process at work in creative dreams, initiation dreams, and even in visitation dreams, where an entity from another dimension seems to enter the dream, giving advice or guidance.[86]

<u>Psychology of Dreams, Western Views</u>

Much has been written about dreams from a psychological perspective. Because it has been documented in depth, and excellent summaries are offered elsewhere by scholars in the field of psychology,[87] I will present only a brief overview in order to provide a framework of how dreams have generally been viewed in the West.

Sigmund Freud reawakened interest in dreams in the West. He referred to dream work as "the royal road to the unconscious." In *The Interpretation of Dreams*, he theorized dreams are essentially a manifestation of repressed wishes and sexual desires. Freud held that each character in the dream represents a condensed symbol that through free association can be exposed. In less recognized lectures published in 1916 on psychoanalysis, Freud acknowledged telepathy in dreaming and the existence of lucid dreaming.[88]

Carl Jung, a student of Freud, could not accept an emphasis on sexual repression. Many of Jung's theories on dreams were based on his experiences with Eastern religions. Jung claimed that a collective unconscious, a type of cultural memory belonging to all people, was accessed during the dream state. He coined the term "archetype," a pervasive idea, image, or symbol that forms part of the collective unconscious, or an original pattern or model from which copies are made; a prototype.[89] He also believed that a compensatory function was at work during dreams to correct personality imbalances. Moreover, if one was intellectual in waking life, a feeling type of dream would provide insight and integration.

The Gestalt school of psychology's founder, Fritz Perls, claimed dreams were necessary for integrating all sectors of the personality. He felt dramatic events in dreams may be projections, and that neurosis was a result of a disowning of the self by projection and / or repression. Thus, through reenactments of dream dramas, a reintegration would be developed leading to self discovery.

24

Opponents to the values of the dream experience in the West include J. Allen Hobson of Harvard Medical School who wrote *The Dreaming Brain.* Hobson proposed there exists a 'dream state generator' located in the brain stem that fires neutrons randomly.[90]

Mytho-Religious Viewpoint on Dreams

Throughout the process of gathering information for this book, it became increasingly evident that more primary research is needed from the viewpoint of dreamers who directly experience the numinous, especially in the field of Mytho-Religious studies. Research of this type is timely and warranted, especially in the West.[91] It could advance the understanding of numinous presence as a guiding force for the development of human potential and spiritual development.

In the East, Buddhist and Bon methods of dream awareness training is purported to span back thousands of years. There is a particular type of spiritual dream called a *Milam Ter* (dream treasures) which are spiritual teachings believed to be created by enlightened beings.[92] Since ancient times, there have been stories about the finding of treasures (*termas*) and meeting of teachers to receive specific teachings or transmissions through dreams. Namkhai Norbu affirms from personal experience that teachers can enter a disciple's dreams and transmit teachings.[93]

According to Serinity Young, specific rituals to the Buddhist goddess Tara clear the way to lucid dreams. A Tangyur text called *Svapna Tara Sadhana,* devoted to Tara, promises to produce prophetic dreams and dreams that lead the way to spiritual realization. According to the text, a sadhana begins with bowing one's head down to the noble dream Tara's feet, requesting a clear dream. This action is performed after a purification of one's body (bathing and perfuming) and mind (arising early with a pure mind). One continues by adorning an image of Tara with offerings, then taking refuge in the three jewels, the Buddha, dharma, and sangha. One then repeats the a mantra for merit and to dispel obstacles to the path during the dream. After the recitation, one meditates to the deity visualizing her in a specific way according to the teachings explicitly detailed. Another mantra is recited and then one is ready to examine the dream.[94]

Why Work with Dreams?

A recurrent question in the literature on dreams is—why work with dreams? Deslauriers asserts working with spiritual insight derived from dreams expands one's boundaries of experiencing, leading to greater authenticity; it cultivates spiritual intelligence.[95] Through attention to the numinous in dreams, he feels we can develop imaginal capacities as adults in order to access spirit. Our imaginal skills have been left to atrophy in the atmosphere of placing emphasis on the mind. Insights from dream study goes beyond the rational to other ways of knowing and knowledge of the heart. Symbols from dreams can "open up dimensions of experience that would otherwise remain closed or hidden or that humans cannot reach through more rational means."[96] It's a matter of understanding the language of dreams, not only relying on our mental faculties.

The Language of Dreams

To understand and deepen a relationship with the dream numen, it is helpful to learn the language of metaphor. Divine guardians and spirit allies speak to us in Spiritually Transformative Dreams, not merely through words, but in signs, symbols, metaphors and humor, and through multi-sensory channels. How we process the information is the key to how we connect with them. By taking the time to give undivided attention to numinous presences in dreams through rituals, gestures, reenactments, creative, expressive arts, we begin to form an alliance with them. A personal language is developed born from responsiveness and interaction.

26

Spiritually Transformative Experiences

Working with dreams as a tool can beneficially affect our lives in transformative ways leading to greater personal growth and spiritual unfoldment, deepen our connections to ancestral roots, and inspire innovative possibilities for the future. Spacious ways of being, seeing, hearing, and communicating experienced in Spiritually Transformative Experiences,[97] including Exceptional Human Experiences[98] and Spiritual Transformative Dreams contribute to the way we see the world. Through dream enactments, we learn about limitless, nurturing possibilities. The numena in our dreams, whether in anthropomorphic or zoomorphic form, or as a shapeshifting force may steer the dreamer to a greater understanding of her or his true nature and calling in life. Through imagery, sound and story line, the numena illustrate, initiate and help us integrate sublime, subtle experiences we may not have had the time to cultivate or even consider, yet are crucial to sensitizing us to the unseen worlds and the wonders of the natural world. By opening to the wisdom teachings of the numena and keeping the skeptical voices at bay by suspending feelings of disbelief, we begin to witness a greater awareness unfold.

Experience of Essence

Ali Hammed Almaas, known for his work on 'essence and personality'[99] conveys that numinous presence is ultimately ineffable, beyond words. Jean Houston also comments on the ineffable experience of essence:

> Perhaps words can describe some aspects of the experiences but only those who truly understand are those who already had or are on the verge of experiencing the numinous . . . Essence is the deepest part of our nature, an actual presence that is innate and inborn. Sometimes it wears a personal face and a form and manifests as an image to our mind's eye. When it does, some call it a 'daimon,' others an angel . . . it is called the 'diamond body' to suggest the crystalline nature of this inner reality. Essence is so real . . . it exceeds all symbols, images, and language. Symbols and images can provide, perhaps, flashes of insight about Essence, but not its living embodied experience. Language fails in its attempts to describe Essence

27

or denote its activities and capacities. Essence, we must conclude can only be experienced. Essence may be the most important requirement for our emergence as full human beings . . . When such moments are accompanied by profound joy, by a sense of blissful and almost supernatural felicity, we can assume that we have touched into Essence. We enter then into a mythic domain in which the extraordinary is ordinary.[100]

The numinous experience enables us to experience our authentic selves. Marcia Sinetar in *Ordinary People as Monks and Mystics* eloquently states:

One is being rather than becoming; she simply directly rests in her authentic self. Even if this experience lasts a mere moment, one's life can be dramatically altered from the union of changing yet non-changing nature of reality and one's place in it as a microcosm of the macrocosm. One's mind stops identification and a merging takes place. This results in a unifying integration where one witnesses all things new again.[101]

Opening to the gifts offered us through numinous dreams, we are provided with fresh new perspectives on how we see ourselves and our relationship to others. We may find ourselves feeling less fragmented, alienated and more connected to the world around us. We begin to feel more whole, integrated, joyful, like a child again, marveling, with a renewed a sense of wonder. Experiential engagement with dream numena brings us closer to an empathetic understanding of our natural environment and our place in it. Our increased sensitivity and compassion to other species is heightened. We are able to viscerally comprehend the fluid energetic *beingness* of all living things, the synergetic network of life. Thus, connecting with numena in dreams—animals, plants, wisdom beings and forces—teaches us to more skillfully co-exist, empathize and participate in healing the environment and creating harmony. To extend this one step further, Stanislav Grof states: "Many years of research have demonstrated that in non-ordinary states of consciousness [i.e., Holotropic Breathwork, dreaming] we cannot only witness mythic and archetypal realities, we can actually become these archetypes."[102]

28

Personal Mythology

Discovery of recurring imagery in dreams may reveal thematic mythic threads that tie to early childhood experiences. Combined with discovered links to ancestral roots gleaned through travel to sacred sites and to one's ancestral lands, a living mythic story can begin to emerge, take shape, then evolve. According to James Hillman, "We must attend very carefully to childhood to catch early glimpses of the *daimon* in action, to grasp its intentions and not block its way."[103] Hillman continues,

> A myth itself is a fractal, a repetition of patterns of becoming. When we reflect on our lives, it is possible to discern repeating themes, and patterns to see the bigger picture. Time is not a linear progression. Rather, it is a fluid medium in which everything is interconnected and time itself may be elemental.[104]

Eastern Views on Dreams

It is believed spiritual transmissions from guides can occur through dreams. Namkhai Norbu affirms from personal experience that teachers can enter a disciple's dreams and transmit teachings. For example, in one dream a dakini presented to him tantras. On another occasion "he dreamt the goddess Tara told him where to find a female ascetic who 'could tell him all that he wished to know.'"[105]

Serinity Young states the Buddhist goddess Tara is considered to be a guide not only in the waking state but in the dream state, as well. Rituals to The Noble Dream Tara include a practice of embodying the deity. "This is accomplished by envisioning oneself as looking like the deity, sounding like the deity through the chanting of a particular mantra, and assuming the deity's mental state . . . ."[106] This method clears the way to lucid dreams.

Since ancient times there have been stories about discoveries of treasures (*termas*), meetings with teachers in dreams. A Tangyur text called *Svapna Tara Sadhana* is devoted to Tara which promises to produce prophetic dreams and dreams that lead the way to spiritual realization. According to the text, a sadhana begins with bowing one's head down to the noble dream Tara's feet, requesting a clear dream. This is preceded with purification procedures (bathing and scenting the body) and preparing the mind, offerings to Tara and taking refuge and specific mantras, visualizations, and recitations. The following is a part of a dream sadhana to Tara.

> From the sky the Noble Lady will spread a cool ray of light rising from her heart and eliminate all the obscurations from one's tormented heart so that it becomes pure like a cloudless sky. Her hands and arms are strong like an elephant's trunk, spreading nectar and pouring down streams of nectar which fill upon one's heart. Through this power one's body becomes very pure like a crystal vessel, cleansed and very beautiful. With a one-pointed and undisturbed mind one should recite the eight syllable mantra *Om Tare Tu Tare Ture* to the superb excellent goddess until one falls asleep in the posture of the sleeping lion.[107]

When one awakens mindful and rested, it is said she / he will remember the dream and see prophetic signs or symbols, perhaps through a teaching or vision.[108]

CHAPTER 3: WAYS OF KNOWING, ESTABLISHING CONNECTIONS OF ENGAGEMENT

At the commencement of this study, my interest in the numinous spanned a wide spectrum. I was drawn to: 1) shamanic healing practices including the accoutrements, ritualistic and initiatory elements; 2) Authentic Movement practice, 3) sacred dance, 4) the female deities of the Buddhist and Hindu traditions, 5) earth-based indigenous practices, 6) folklore and mythology of the sacred woman, and 7) the phenomena of dreams and the ancient practices of dream incubation. How I was going to narrow it down to a workable project presented quite a challenge. I found the focus could be approached in a number of different ways. It was clear the method would dictate and shape the direction I would follow during the course of the investigation so it was vital I designed one that would strongly anchor the study.

When looking for a methodology that would best suit this work on my experiences with numena in dreams, I set out by reviewing research methods I was familiar with and those that resonated with my worldview. I had taken graduate courses in both Organic Inquiry and Heuristic Methods and was impressed with these innovative autobiographical approaches to research and focuses on transformation.

Organic Inquiry

Organic Research interested me ever since I first heard about it. It is a relatively new method (1994) initially pioneered by five women: Jennifer Clements, Dorothy Ettling, Dianne Jenett, Nora Taylor, and Lisa Fields. They were seeking a more inclusive method of inquiry, one that included the personal experiences of the researcher, the spiritual features and ideology based on feminine spirituality, chthonic and liminal experiences, narratives, stories, and transformative change.[109] Jennifer Clements defines this method,

> Organic inquiry is a qualitative research approach for the study of topics relating to psycho-spiritual growth, in which one's psyche becomes the subjective instrument

of the research, working in partnership with liminal and spiritual sources as well as with participants who have had related experiences. Analysis, which involves the cognitive integration of liminal encounters, results in transformative changes to the researcher's understanding and experience of the topic. These are changes of mind and heart, which both inform and transform. In presenting the results, the researcher uses stories to invite the individual reader to a parallel, yet unique, transformative experience.[110]

In Organic Inquiry, five steps of research are explained metaphoric to growing a plant: 1) the soil is first prepared (a clearing of the mind to allow for an openness to the unimaginable); then, 2) the seed is planted (the researcher's story is shared); 3) the roots emerge (trusting in the process, allowing it freedom to emerge on its own); 4) the tree begins to grow (inviting participation from co-researchers, branching out to understand the wider cultural significances). Finally, 5) the fruit is harvested (transformation is realized leading to an increased awareness of self, spirit and service to others).

All modes of experience are valued as pertinent to Organic Inquiry—not only through intellect but visceral, intuitive, chthonic, somatic, mental, emotional, psychic, and spiritual modes. In fact, what attracted me most about this methodology was its platform on claiming research as sacred. It was the only methodology I found that addressed spiritual issues. As a long time Buddhist (I have followed the tenets of Buddhism since I first picked up the book, *The Way of Zen* by Alan Watts[111] when I was fourteen), I wanted a method that would allow me to focus on my spiritual path.

Organic Inquiry's foundation, built from the contributions of scholars in the fields of Women's Spirituality and Transpersonal Psychology also resonated with me. I received a M.A. in Humanities with a concentration in Women's Spirituality so found it was in line with my feminist perspectives. As an woman in midlife, brought up in the fifties and sixties, I believe women's personal stories need to be told, written by women in the first person singular; that correctives of deletions, under-valuations and marginalization of women's creative, spiritual and intellectual contributions need to be addressed and expressed.[112] I consider feminism a process committed to life- affirming

32

ways to preserve and enhance the quality of life for all living beings and things. It rallies the causes for freedom for all oppressed groups and is concerned with the development of interconnections and relationships.

After reading the autobiographical works of Dr. Lucia Birnbaum, I was especially drawn to use Organic Methods. Professor Birnbaum's work focuses on the subaltern perspective,[113] women's empowerment and women's autobiographical accounts.[114] Her stance rallying the significance of learning about one's ancestral roots had a life-changing effect on me. Both her books, *The Black Madonna* and *Dark Mother* exemplify the autobiographical process as a transformative process. I began to realize the impact of writing the personal story. In Organic Inquiry, Dorothy Clements remarks, "Having one's story completely heard changes one,"[115] It changes the writer and the reader. I began to understand its wider transformative ramifications.

I tried to imagine myself writing with the intention of revealing my innermost thoughts and musings. Generally, I am a private person so this seemed like quite a challenge for me. I also am not a journal or letter writer. Spending an immense amount of time thinking about and conceptualizing feelings, intuitions, and sensations into words is usually less enjoyable to me than simply relaxing, listening to the sound of the birds and just being. So, I wondered, why would I want to choose a method that required personal disclosure and journal writing as fundamental aspects? Deep in my heart, I knew that I wanted to get to the roots of things—a kind of roots housecleaning at midlife. But, at the beginning of the investigation, I could not articulate clearly what it was I needed to find out about my self that I didn't already know. What did I need polished? Were there skeletons in my closet? To get to the very roots of the roots meant that I had to dig deeper, travel to a place of my heritage where my ancient grandmothers lived.

The method needed to evolve naturally, formed through an interaction with the numen (the sacred presences were my co-researchers in this investigation) before, during, and after the study. My intent was to negotiate a connection with the numena, to work toward relationship, to "place a foot in both worlds" using all ways of knowing. Also, I was especially concerned with preserving the integrity of the numena. They were living presences to me and it was important they weren't treated as merely objects or specimens in a research study.

Thus, applying modified versions of Organic Inquiry methods (in particular the sacred and autobiographical elements), I drew on my inner authority, stood at the center of my own experience, and invited a co-emergence to develop between the wisdom guides in my dreams, myself and my personal story—an inter-inspirational endeavor. I also borrowed Organic Inquiry's allowance for an intuitive approach when synthesizing the findings, one that would permit the spirit of the study to naturally find its own method of integration and closure.

Heuristic Inquiry

In addition to adopting some of the elements of Organic Inquiry, I used modified versions of a few steps in Heuristic Inquiry.

The root meaning of *heuristic* comes from the Greek word *heuriskein*, meaning to discover, or to find. It refers to a process of internal search by which one discovers the nature and meaning of a kind of experience. Clark Moustakis developed Heuristic Inquiry as a response to influences from Abraham Maslow's work on "self-actualization," Jourand's work on "self-disclosure," the works of Michael Polyani, Eugene Gendlin, Martin Buber, P. Bridgman, and Carl Rogers.[116] It is essentially a method that accepts and encourages investigations of non-rational experiences.[117]

When the method of Heuristic Inquiry is used, the researcher is the focus, present throughout the entire process, thus the personal story is of prime importance. The topic becomes one's life while the question or topic is being studied. A wide range of research materials (including relevant and sometimes lengthy illustrative passages from textual sources and those derived from creative processes—art, journaling, poetry, and story) are allowed to broaden the understanding of the phenomena under investigation. As

34

understanding of the intricacies of the phenomena increases during the study, the researcher experiences growing self-awareness and self-knowledge.[118]

Beginning with a profound experience (the researcher must have had direct experience with the topic under investigation), she or he participates in a process that begins with: 1) "initial engagement" (finding a topic of critical interest using self dialogue, intuition, "felt sense;" 2) "immersion" (letting the topic live in all aspects of one's life so that an expansion has room to occur); 3) "incubation" when one disengages from the research, lets go of the intense concentration. Often it is during these times elucidations appear as if out of nowhere; 4) "illumination," occurrences which bring new light to the topic; 5) "explication," the point in the investigation where one delves into the research using all modes of inquiry (intuition, "felt sense," intellectual, somatic, etc.). The final phase of Heuristic Inquiry is 6) the "creative synthesis," results of the inquiry in the form of a narrative, poem or other creative means, a creative expression that sums up the essence of the study.

I use the term immersion differently in this study. It is the first phase in the method design (Immersion Phase) in which I identify and select the numen by way of reading the dreams. Another difference is that I the use the term amplification instead of explication for the phase of research (Amplification Phase) when I am exploring mytho-religious and personal connections to the dream numena.

Similarities and differences between Organic Inquiry and Heuristic Inquiry are: 1) Heuristic methods subscribe to the hermeneutics of self-discovery.[119] Similarly, Organic Inquiry centers on personal transformation through a "looking within;" 2) Heuristic Inquiry aims toward a synthesis of data and seems to be more concentrated on topics of experiences of fear, courage, nature, whereas Organic Inquiry tends to be more about how individuals experience their bodies; it is more spiritually and relationship oriented; 3) Heuristic is more abstract, theoretical and inward, whereas Organic is more relational and invites participation from the reader; 4) Heuristic gives suggestions step by step, while Organic encourages the researcher to design her own method; 5) As mentioned,

Organic Inquiry clearly envisions research as sacred. Even though in Heuristic Inquiry Moustakis doesn't mention spiritual, or sacred, it is implied. Both Organic and Heuristic work with co-researchers. In this work the numena are considered in this role.

This study, therefore, is approached from my point of view as a spiritual archaeologist / artist / pilgrim who attempts to focus on (with introspective sensitivity, care and attention) dream numena that have regularly visited me in dreams. The research design I use is a blend of modified versions of Heuristic Inquiry, and Organic Inquiry, methodologies that support the non-linear, unfolding, sacred, creative, and transformative aspects of self-discovery. The flexibility of this method allows for a living, breathing process to emerge over time, which may even include a change of direction and structure, if needed. Both Heuristic Inquiry and Organic Inquiry (in comparison to other qualitative methodologies)[120] herald this organic process of investigation. Through a reimagining of the numen and numinous (putting aside any notions of their unreality), and through surrendering, trust and faith, my intentions are to open to their guidance, protection, and healing. In many instances, I follow a "right-brained" process.[121] Three phases toward integration include: 1) Immersion Phase (identifying the numena), 2) Amplification Phase (meeting the numena) and 3) Engagement Phase (engaging with the numena).

The Steps of the Research

In describing the design I have created, I will begin with an explanation of each phase and my purposes for choosing these steps. The results of this method are described in Chapter 8.

Finding the Topic

It seems easy enough to think that choosing a topic is just deciding on something that one has developed interest in over the years and developing a plan to investigate it. This isn't always the case, especially when one has a wide range of interests. Techniques to center in on what holds the most transformative possibilities are often used. Organic

Inquiry, in fact, specifically places more attention on designating a place of entry into the study rather than just picking something randomly and following a structured set of procedures to follow every course of the way.

An effective method of finding topic themes is through self-dialogue: stream-of-thought writing, journaling, focusing, and clustering.

The process of *focusing*[122] helps to center in on a topic. Steps of focusing include: going inward to find the essence of thoughts and feelings in clarifying a question, then "'getting a handle on it,'" looking at its parts, themes, sub-themes; looking deeply for what has the most *juice*, removing extraneous materials in order to focus more completely. The main point is that it *"enables the researcher to identify qualities of an experience that have remained out of conscious reach primarily because the individual has not paused long enough to examine his or her experience of the phenomenon"* [my italics].[123] In summary, it requires six steps: 1) clearing a space, 2) the felt sense, 3) finding a handle, 4) resonating, 5) asking, and, 6) receiving.

I also try *clustering*[124] possible topics and subtopics. Known to be highly effective for organizing research materials, clustering involves writing a key word in the center of a large piece of paper (newsprint art paper works well for this). Using the word as a nucleus, I branch out with free associative words, then group them into themes. I call it the "spidering" technique as that it often resembles a spider's web when the process is completed.

Pace

At the beginning of the study, I decide not to rush into it, to be aware of any signs from synchronistic events, conversations, observations, intuitions, and trust that a succinct topic will formulate on its own accord, that it will reveal itself. One enters into the study with the knowledge it requires patience and sustained immersion for sake of clarity and for transformation to develop on its own accord.

37

Experimentations

Another method that may be used for finding the topic of inquiry is the "Experimentations." This is a timely process (it may include fieldwork) and one must be willing to 'try topics on for size,' risking that most or all the research collected might not be incorporated into the final work. The positive results of this step, however, is that through a deeper involvement with possible themes, one is able to get a clear picture if the topic will lend itself for sustained interest for the long haul.[125] Other beneficial outcomes are that one learns more about research techniques, areas of personal and academic interests, and has collected research material for further investigations, courses, lectures, workshops, articles, art shows, etc. "Experimentations" leads to self-discoveries but does require that one doesn't get diverted by tangential materials.

The Topic Ritual

The topic has been chosen. Next, a ritual is created to mark the beginning of the study. This is time to take a moment for celebration. One approaches the time ahead with a beginner's mind "an attitude . . . [of] wonder, enjoyment, surprise, playfulness, awe, and deep appreciation."[126] A ritual of honoring and invoking the numena marks the entry into the study. Since my topic focuses on the spirit guardians of my dreams, I invite Tara, the 'crossing over' goddess. I present this opening ritual in the Prologue. I choose a time of year of boundary crossings, May Day, or "Maia Day," the day of the Mother.

Immersion Phase

I am familiar with numinous content in imaginal work not only through shamanic journey practice and work with entheogens but through other methods of communing with the spirit world. During Authentic movement practices, I interact with geometric shapes, eggs, lotus deities, snakes, birds, flowers, rainbows. In Holotropic Breathwork, I experienced profound prenatal epiphanies born from numinous content. In both these practices, one is awake, though in a trance state. In dreams, too, one is in a liminal dream

38

space where a range of numinous experiences can be engaged in (flying, mergings, receiving healings and transmissions from deer, lions and angelic beings, etc., similar to journeying—entheogenic, and otherwise).

In the immersion phase, the dreams are collected, read several times, titled, and entered into a database. Then, I highlight a word or sets of words that evoke a *charge*— words that describe characters, scenes, sounds and images that I remember were particularly pronounced and vivid, dynamic, mysterious, uplifting, perplexing, unusual, blissful. From the highlighted dreams, I select those according to patterns that emerged, frequency of numinous occurrences, personal interest and "felt sense."

After periods of incubation (breaks from the study to allow for relaxation from concentrated attention which often spurs more insight), I further refine the list of dreams. Then, I pick three dream numena for the study, 1) the "Spirit of Sound," the "Mother," and the "Skywoman" numena) and three dream types (*Clarity dreams*, *Personal Mythology dreams*, and *Initiation dreams*). The types of dreams correspond to the major themes I am curious to explore, i.e., the "Spirit of Sound" will be studied through a juxtaposition of *Clarity dreams*, the "Mother" in *Personal Mythology dreams*, and the" Skywomen" numena through *Initiation dreams*.

Clarity dreams highlight the essence of the connection, concentrating on how the numen was received. Personal Mythology dreams highlight the dream experiences that illuminate, support and encourage the on-going shaping of the researcher's "mythic" story. And, Initiation dreams highlight the lessons learned, gifts offered, transmissions, empowerments given by way of divine intervention.

Amplification Phase

"The complexity of the researcher as the human instrument has only begun to be explicated."[127]To allow the outer, or historical, meaning to reflect back on and illuminate the more obscure personal symbolism is what Carl Jung called "amplification." Beverly Moon in *An Encyclopedia of Archetypal Symbolism* states:

When one of Jung's patients reported the appearance in a dream of an unusual (especially a numinous, that is, awe-inspiring) symbol, Jung would first ask for personal associations. Next, he would turn to the writings of the historians of religions to find the meaning of the image within a specific cultural context. Historical amplification of subjective material serves to deepen the patient's understanding of the inner experience. Very often such amplification facilitated the healing of some subjective wound, because seeing one's own dilemma in terms of a universal drama can connect the person to the roots of his or her humanity and to the inner resources that have the power to resolve conflicts while engendering new attitudes and new life.[128]

In this second phase, I use techniques of amplification to initially look for personal associations. Then, I turn to historical and mythic source materials derived from the research of cultural historians, artists and healers. The process is akin to turning up the volume or focusing the lens on individual and broader aspects while a gestalt is being formed.

Heuristic Methods uses creative imagination to illustrate points made. The use of excerpts or entire passages from documents, correspondence, records, poems, letters, journal entries, artwork, artifacts, and open ended interviews are encouraged—anything that can further illuminate the focus of the investigation is used. These are included throughout this book, as well as in Appendix B, but particularly in the amplification phase of the work. The Amplification Phase is where the "getting to know," or "meeting" the spirit guides occurs. It is allowed to evolve on its own terms through whatever emerges, i.e., literary, artistic, poetic, mythic, reflective modes.

The researcher is the vehicle, the witness, and midwife, the "light that guides."[129] During this phase, focusing, "felt sense," reflection, journaling, clustering, self-dialogue, textual research, internet research, meditation, walking, use of aromatherapy, Tibetan Bon spiritual practices, conversations, open-ended interviews and guidance from colleagues may be employed, as well.

Again, periods of incubation—a withdrawal from everyday life, a relaxation or retreat from concentrated focus is incorporated. I choose walks in nature, beach walks, going to boundary places. Activities such as note-taking or reading are suspended in order to allow for a further amplification and more subtle, delicate understandings of the dream numena in preparation for the Engagement Phase to emerge. It allows for new dimensions of experience, awakenings of insights previously not comprehended to be experienced, as well as breakthroughs borne from surrender, trust and openness.

Engagement Phase

In phase three, I re-enter the dream through "active imagination."[130] I engage in any means that best connects me to the sacred message, story line or numena in order to be with the sacred image or force. It is the place of tender communication. A ritual, artwork, whatever best suits engagement with the numena is enacted or created.

Method of Analysis: Compassionate Knowing

Along with Intuitive Analysis of Organic Methods, I use the function of "Compassionate Knowing"[131] to determine the outcome of this investigation. Compassionate Knowing is based on the supposition that to know a thing requires loving it—to look within the phenomena enables one "be with it," to truly engage with it.

> Compassionate knowing has a softness. It is as if what is observed yields itself to our knowing. There is no intrusion, no object, and no subject. Aspects of the experience studied that do not belong to the depth of the experience fall away. Those aspects that give amplitude and fullness to the experience studied begin to cohere in their complexity and interrelatedness (interbeingness). By loving, and through living thoroughly the experience studied, the researcher looks around from the inside the experience until the essential qualities of the experience come to life as the researcher's own experience. Gradually, the entire panorama of the experience comes more clearly into view.[132]

Practices

Throughout the process or this work, I engaged in the following practices to enhance all phases of the investigation: meditation, walking, journaling, gardening, aromatherapy, salt baths, and massage. I attended teachings by Lamas, Bon Masters in meditation retreats; rituals with an *Ialorixa* of the Afro-Brazilian tradition of Umbanda. Periodically, I engaged in shamanic journeys. Frequently, I listened to spiritual music, Tibetan singing bowls and towards the end of the study, began to study Nada Yoga.[133] I viewed artifacts, adornments, relics, amulets, and statuary related to numena in books and in museum collections. I attended workshops and lectures on related topics. Studies included: fieldwork, library research, internet research, viewing of videotapes, and listening to conversations and interviews with shamans, curenderas, sound healers, Lamas, bodyworkers, aromatherapists, artists, intuitives, museum curators, psychologists, tantric Buddhist and Hindu practitioners, *devis*, authors, and healers. Toward the beginning of the study, I arranged for blessing pujas to be held for me in Kathmandu, Nepal by two holy women, Kusali Devi and the *kumari* of Bhaktapur.

The oracular tools I worked with included: The tarot, runes, Medicine Cards, I-Ching, the oracular as found in nature,[134] and shamanic oracular methods. I generally withdrew from an active social life between July 2002 and October 2003. During nine months of this investigation, I underwent feminist Buddhist counseling in weekly sessions, working with dreams, sandtray, Authentic Movement,[135] aromatherapy, breathwork, and visualizations.

Natural Language

Considering this study is intended for a wider audience interested in one Western woman's spiritual path and point of view, a natural language is what I have chosen to use in contrast to academic language. This is in line with the tenets of Organic Inquiry. As Dorothy Clements states, "The vernacular is intended to reach a wider audience."[136] I recall the words of Dr. Cindy Shearer when she reminded me, "The personal is universal."[137] This style is also encouraged in Heuristic Methods in which the voice of the primary researcher is allowed full expression. Any term that I think needs further explanation or clarification is included in the Glossary or Notes.

CHAPTER 4: INTRODUCTION TO THE DREAMS

First I recount the dream. If it is one sequence in a series of dreams, I include the entire dream series (or parts) in order to further understand the mythopoeic content and to provide a sense of continuity. After presenting the dreams, an amplification is offered containing mytho-religious associations and reflections, feelings, personal perspectives and / or ideas that arose during the recollection of the dreams and research. Carl Jung believed that by applying this method of amplification—exploring symbolism, personal intuitions, any information that can amplify elements of the dream for further contemplation—layers of archetypal meanings and deeper connections unfold.

Next, through engagement practices, the dreamer forms a bond and interacts with the numena. During this phase a ritual honoring the numena of the particular dream using a symbolic action is performed. Acknowledgement and expressions of gratitude are offered which may include: material offerings and / or sacred gestures, behaviors, i.e., mudras, singing, sounding, dancing, movement, etc. Embodiment practices that bridge the realms of the dreams to the dreamer in waking consciousness expand her or his world view. Hence, "experiences we gain from practices we do during our dream time can then be brought into our daytime experience."[138] We develop balance, a sense of integration, and flexibility due to our embodied comprehension of our interconnectedness.

> With continuing practice we see less and less difference between the waking and the dream state. Our experiences in waking life become more vivid and varied, the result of a lighter and more refined awareness . . . This kind of awareness, based on dream practice, can help create an inner balance. Awareness nourishes the mind in a way that nurtures the whole living organism."[139]

Eventually with practice, according to *The Doctrine of the Dream State*, an ancient Tibetan text on dream yoga, the advanced practitioner is able to become a bird, a lion, change size, fly to mystical lands, etc.[140] The dreamer becomes the vehicle. And, through experiential understanding of our bonds with all species, we learn greater compassion.

CHAPTER 5: SINGING WITH SHIVA:
ENGAGING WITH THE SOUND NUMENA

Sound Dreams

5-7-00 merging

I am asked to read a short passage over the radio waves. I sound each individual word as if it is a song, mantra, or seed syllable and produce a divine-like, other-worldly vibrational tone. I feel transported, ecstatic, as well as somewhat astounded that this sound is coming from me.

1-17-03 the play

I am a little late entering the theater. I sit down with a couple friends, have a good seat and a good view. My ex-husband is going to be in the play. Some people in the audience are given special mantras and tablets to eat for a later designated time. The tablets have something etched on them in Sanskrit. During curtain time (intermission), those chosen recite their mantras and eat the tablets. After I chant then eat mine, I begin to rise up in the air. I keep rising and rising until I am above the clouds. When I look down, everything is so astoundingly beautiful. I am filled with bliss. I am getting a little nervous because I am so high up. I realize it's just all in my mind. The fear is just a projection of my mind. Then, I feel self-assured to enjoy and be up there, up high, enjoying this experience.

1-21-03 Shiva's shrine

I am in India and a fatherly man is teaching me. He is telling me that I have a blue aura. He sketches a picture of me sitting in a meditation posture. Then with an azure blue crayon draws in rays of blue to depict my energy field. He tells me, "Yes, your aura is blue."

next scene: *A woman and man teach me Indian dance movements forming mudras with my hands. There are others in the class (held outdoors) practicing mudras, as well. I let go. My arms move on their own and take on their own energy; they feel like snakes. I observe this in wonder and curiosity.*

next scene: *The woman and man cut an outfit for me out of a shimmery golden Indian material. Then, the man gives me some clay and shows me how to work with it forming it from the middle out. I can see the person next to me has created some kind of scene with his clay.*

next scene: *I am walking in a temple setting in a place that looks like Kathmandu. An unidentifiable animal in a pear tree comes down and begins to follow me. I am instructed mentally not to make eye contact with it, to ignore it and it will turn around and go away which it does. I walk along the path and come upon Shiva's shrine—a statue of Shiva inside an open temple where there is a place to rest my forehead. I bow down and begin to recite the mantra to Shiva . . ."Om Nama Shivaya." I enter into a deep devotional trance.*

Amplification on the Spirit of Sound Numena

I begin by choosing aspects in the preceding dreams that stand out most prominently in relation to characteristics of clarity: 1) the numinous quality of sound, 2) the mantra, and 3) the shrine of Shiva. In order to comprehend the gestalt of the dreams, I look for any immediate connections. Right away I notice: 1) the Indian meditator / teacher shares the same posture as Shiva, the Yogi. 2) In the first dream (5-7-00 merging), I recall the voice fills me, resonates through my being as if awakening and brightening every cell. In the third dream (1-21-03 Shiva's shrine) the mantra is experienced as a transporter, a formless numen or force. The vibrational energy of the sound is not contained solely within my body but is extended outwards into an aura of sound around me. It is a magnificent sound, a sound I hear only in my dreams. I awake in a sense of awe, wonder, and deep gratitude. The message of the dreams is apparent—to open to the fullness of the experience of pure sound resonance. That is the message, to be present with it and to accept it as a healing and a gift.

Having experienced the numen of sound on several occasions in dream states (again, not as a reified entity but rather as a vibrational force) has inspired me to investigate this phenomena further. Focusing on the quality of the sound, I think back on a lecture and demonstration on Nada Yoga given by Silvia Nakkach, a world-wide accredited specialist in cross-cultural music therapy and sound healing, composer and founder of the Vox Mundi School. Silvia explained how techniques of sound toning facilitate a purification, magnetization, activation and balancing of the chakras. While working with the voice, each note is meant to correspond to a particular emotion. When practiced correctly, one is able to release repressed emotions and become receptive to subtle vibrations leading to healing of the body and mind. By using techniques of Nada Yoga, a person is also able to discover one's own natural voice, or tone that resonates for her or him.

Recently I met with Silvia again at a meditation retreat and asked her if she had heard about the phenomena of hearing sound in dreams. She affirmed that she had. It was her view that if one "sounded" (sang, chanted, worked with the voice) more in waking life, most likely experiences of sound in dreams would lessen then eventually diminish. This presented a conundrum to me as I didn't wish to lose the capacity to hear what I can only describe as "the sound of the spheres" in dream states yet I also wished to connect with these sounds while in waking consciousness. I felt the numena of sound in my dreams were calling me to engage with them on a deeper level. I am a private person and dream space offered a comfortable environment for me, a safe haven to feel entirely free to express vocal expressions, sounds, feelings and other sensual expressions. However, it was becoming clear I needed to engage with expressions of the numena of sound in both dreaming *and* waking, one informing the other. I began to explore sound techniques that produced supra-subtle vibrational tones (overtone chanting, singing bowls, throat singing,

46

Nada Yoga). I also became aware that I needed to explore Dream Yoga in order to sharpen my attention while dreaming.

I continued to research the practice of Nada Yoga. Yogi Hari, direct heir of Swami Nadabrahmananda, one of the last great Nada Yoga Masters informs us about its effects,

> The Mystics and Yogis have used this principle of vibration in the realm of music to harmonize their gross physical body and subtle body in order to reconnect to the primordial source. Nada Yoga represents the technical vibratory aspect of the sacred chants (Mantras, Bhajans, Kirtans) which, through its positive vibrations, harmonises our physical and 'astral' bodies (energy, emotions, intellect), and in so doing gives us a glimpse of our "causal" body, the deepest part of ourselves whose nature is peace. This harmonisation eliminates many physical and mental tensions. Nada Yoga ultimately leads us back to the source of creation by using sound vibration . . . [Steps in this process include:] listening to and chanting Mantras, Bhajans, Kirtans whose vibrations are pure because they have been composed and are interpreted by yogis, saints, etc. This practice cleanses the mind and impregnates positive impressions. . . This pure music stabilises our attention, calms the mind and renders the adept sensitive to more subtle frequencies, enabling him [or her] to hear 'Anahata.' This internal sound comes from the vibration of prana [life force]. . . The mind, absorbed in this 'Anahata' is in a transcendental state. It experiences the Absolute, or God as 'Nadam' pure vibration.[141]

Continuing my research on sound in dreams, I met with friend, composer and recording artist Steven Halpern and asked if he had heard about hearing sound in dreams. He informed me that indeed he had. Steven experienced the sound of bells and "floating phrases" in dreams preceding and during the time of his first recording "Spectrum Suite" back in the early seventies.[142] His sensitivity and development to the subtle vibrational qualities of sound is evident in the many recordings he has since produced.

It became clear that little research was available on sound in dreams. Soon, I discovered the work of Sven Doehner, Ph.D., MFA, a psychotherapist in private practice in Mexico City who worked for many years with native Mexican healers, and guided dream-work groups in Brazil, Greece, Lithuania, Peru, Mexico, the Soviet Union, the U.S.A. and Uruguay. An innovator in alchemical dream-sharing, he works at the borders between contemporary depth psychotherapy and ancient healing traditions. Sven responded to my request for information on sound in dreams by kindly sending me his article, "Sound Transformation in Dream-Work," as well as communicating with me about the topic via email and telephone. In his essay, Sven speaks of sensitizing oneself to the spectral elements contained in the voice. He suggested to listen to the qualities of sound in a person's voice, "the tone, pitch, attitude, extension, height, depth, rhythm, melody, volume, timbre, resonance, dissonance, energy or intention revealed in the sound."[143]

Next, to investigate the energetic, somatic qualities of sound further, I read about the throat chakra, the fifth chakra called the *Visuddha* which also corresponds to the sense of hearing.[144] The challenge of the fifth chakra is to release our fear of communicating and interacting with the world. When we are able to release our fears, sense of powerlessness and pride, we are able to speak our truth confidently and courageously. This chakra is associated with aligning with our intuition which guides us in an optimal flow resulting in seeing our goals manifest. This is the first level of consciousness in which we perceive directly another level of intelligence and experience our interaction with this other intelligence. This chakra functions as the crossover between the physical world and the world of spirit. On the physical level, it corresponds to deep space as the most subtle physical element and is associated with the color sky blue or azure blue. Blockage in this area is indicated by frequent sore throats, swollen glands, colds, thyroid problems and difficulty communicating. For opening the *Visuddha*, there are remedies. It is helpful to sing, chant, hum and breathe consciously.

In Tibetan Buddhism, the throat chakra is associated with the dream state of consciousness. Both Tibetans and Taoists work with this chakra to access the dream state and develop the faculty of lucid dreaming. It is believed to represent the connection between the heart and the third eye.

A gifted, intuitive healer shared with me that in a past life I was well known for healing with my voice (a technique currently unheard of, lost in antiquity) and many people would come to me for healings. She also informed me that in other lifetimes, I rarely spoke and primarily attended to shrines in caves. This information both intrigued and resonated with me. It inspired further research into techniques of sound and ancient instruments. I was particularly interested in the lute and bells, (as well as the frame drum, rattle, and tambourine).

In *The Genius of China,* Robert Temple informs us the Chinese developed a sophisticated understanding of sound and created bells from a variety of metals to produce particular tones and overtones (similar to the concept of Tibetan singing bowls). Playing the *ch'en* or *zither* (related to Saraswati's *vina*) or lute (refined in the third century A.D.) demonstrated their profound understanding of timbre or subtle quality of sound (since equal tempered music, we have been deprived of pure tones). The tonal changes in the voice of the singer would be aligned with the sound of the instrument. There was an "infinite subtlety with which any given note could be played."[145] I have found the singing voice of Silvia Nakkach to contain this element of glorious sensitivity to tone and texture, producing the *rasa* of delight.

Rasa is the essence of an aesthetic experience, a powerful emotional experience often producing sublime pleasure. When listening to ancient Hindu music of the Drupa tradition, for instance, one can be induced into higher states of consciousness. Reflecting on my sound dreams I wonder, is this what my being craves—a connection to the subtle music of the spheres and the need absorb and express the rasa of delight?

During the past decade, dreams of chanting mantras in ritualistic settings have occurred.[146] According to Silvia Nakkach,

> Mantras serve as auditory centering devices which have the power to protect, purify, and transform the emotional and consciousness states of the individual who repeats them. Mantra chanting usually induces devotion in the mind of the singer, activating a state of blissful liberation through sound.[147]

Concentrating on the third sound dream, 1-21-03 "Shiva's shrine" in which I am chanting to Shiva, I begin by examining the symbolism associated with Shiva. I

49

investigate the Sanskrit meaning of *Om Nama Shivaya* and discuss the power of mantras in general.

Shiva, formerly known as Rudra, the Wild God (according to the Rg Veda, 1200 B.C.) is also called the Lord of the Dance. His dance is a form of his being; it is one of bliss called *anandatandava*, a fierce dance performed at dusk in which he dances to the music of the gods. Shiva speaks of himself as the god who sets everything in motion and is always dancing, absorbed in yoga, enjoying supreme bliss. Dance-induced beatitude shines from the faces of many images of Shiva, Lord of Yogis, King of Dancers. There is another aspect of Shiva, *Ardhanarisvara* (the divine androgyny, perfect and whole of itself), half male and half female. Shiva's feminine aspect is referred to as the 'Lady of the Mountain' (Parvati, Rhea, or Cybele), also called the 'White Lady' (Gauri or Leucothea).[148] The followers of the cult of Shiva (*bhaktas*) in India, like the cult of Dionysus (*bacchoi*) in Greece, believed the path to god was through direct communication—through experiences of love and ecstasy.[149] Danielou explains the tenets of Shivaism,

> It is the principle of Shivaism that nothing exists in the whole universe which is not a part of the divine body and which cannot be a way of reaching the divine. All objects, all natural phenomena, plants and animals, as well as aspects of man himself, may be starting points to bring us nearer to the divine. Thus there is neither high nor low, inferior or superior function, sacred or profane. If we recognize the divine order in all our tendencies, all our physical functions, and in all our actions or potential, we become masters of ourselves, companions (*kaula*) of the god, and participants (*bhaktas* or *bacchants*).[150]

I learn that "Om Nama Shivaya" means "Om, to Shiva I bow." This is one of the chief mantras used by Hindus for purposes of attaining spiritual realization, worldly achievement, protection and courage.[151] Mantra means "thought form."[152] It is said that mantras are highly condensed forms of vibrational presence. They are sacred utterances to worship the deity. Mantras are considered identical to the deity in sound form. "The power of the deity is inherent in its name, its formula, its mantra, which becomes the

50

subtle vehicle through which contacts can be established between deity and worshiper."[153] It acts as a vehicle or link between the worlds of spirit and matter.

Layne Redmond (known for her work with the tambourine and frame drum) tells us about the mantra *Aum* pronounced "Om."

> The primal mantra Aum is considered the seed syllable of created existence. This mantra and its sound are linked to the Bindu, the pulse of consciousness, the great beehive—the place of sacred utterance and the buzzing vibration of life. Chanted correctly, it vibrates the cranium and the cerebral cortex of the brain, causing a sound similar to the humming of bees. In yogic practices, the sound of bees buzzing is the closest sound that we can actually hear to the unstruck sound behind reality. . . The Maha Devi, Kundalini, manifests as a queen bee surrounded by bees known as Bhramaridevi, who awakens in a buzz of ascending consciousness and descending spiritual grace. This ascending buzzing energy illuminates the chakras which are interconnected with areas of the brain that are silent in the unawakened state. The brain explodes into awareness as these dormant areas are activated . . . Bhramari, a pranayama practice [is] derived from the buzzing of bees which vibrates and realigns the entire nervous system, brain and body by buzzing the vocal chords.[154]

The Bauls of Bengal are a group of mystic minstrels with a tradition that goes back to ancient times. They sing of communion with the Divine and believe that it can be felt in the body. Mostly poor and country peoples, their songs describe secular expressions of reverie, freedom and joy with the use of poetry and hidden language. Their songs evoke passion and pleasure often with erotic sentiment. Their enigmatic language is called *sandhya* or "twilight language" where the meaning of a word or phrase is hidden in analogy.

In my research I discover the "dakini language" in Vajrayana Buddhism, also called "twilight language" was originally inspired by the goddess Vac[155] later transformed to Saraswati, known to be connected to divine sound.[156] The "Song of the Vajra" is a chant said to be in the dakini language whose sounds vibrate in the body. It is believed to bring waves which "massage the vibrations of the being, bringing an integration with spherical sounds of the universe."[157] June Campbell asserts the dakini

51

language is a metaphor for divine transcendence which is transmitted through the female body, and in particular through the female voice of the dakini.[158] Sometimes the dakini exclude words altogether and transmits teaching directly into one's mind.[159] Reflecting on this I ponder, is it possible I could be receiving teachings via the twilight language? The concept of the dakini will be revisited in Chapter 7 when I discuss the background of the skywomen numena.

Much can be written on the topic of sacred sound in relation to the shaman's song whose rhythmic incantations are the 'boat' to help transport those on a transformative journey. But, I forego discussing this topic in detail as it is beyond the scope of this investigation.

Engagement with the Sound Numena

Shiva ritual: 7-22-03

Today I drive to find a location to honor and commune with Shiva, one of my dream numena of sound. Surrendering myself to the moment, I just drive, letting myself by guided to a destination where hopefully I can find privacy. I am compelled to head towards the ocean. While driving, I remind myself to reside in the present moment, not to anticipate or project how the numen will manifest. I drive pass the border of Sonoma / Marin. I think, "now I am in the 'borderlands,' so must be getting closer." I have driven miles and am getting a little anxious in anticipation and impatience as I don't like to drive. I stay aware for any signs, feelings, observations that will lead me to the ritual site. Up ahead on the right there is an inviting mountain road that is off the beaten path. I look within to observe my response of curiosity, wonder, adventure and understand, yes, I am to take this road. Ascending, I pass a pasture of cows, then further, a meadow of sheep. The landscape changes to greener rolling hills, vistas of the valley below. I park the car near the summit, light the stick of juniper incense I brought along to remind myself of the sacred temples in the Kathmandu Valley in Nepal and smoke some herbs in a small red pipe. I know Shiva is associated with ganja (as well as datura) recalling the sadhus in

Nepal and India. I look out over a vista to the pastel blue lake beyond. From the various CDs I bring, I choose to listen to *The Sacred Chants of Shiva from the Banks of the Ganges.*[160] I decide I will listen to the entire CD. I gaze around at the valley below. A black hawk soars above to the sound of the chanting. Another bird begins to sing. I hear it through my headphones. A yellow butterfly passes in front of me. I breathe the refreshing air, let it clear and purify me as I deeply inhale. I imagine myself a bird as I sit on the hood of my black Honda on top of this mountain. The wind blows through me. A man in a red t-shirt passes me on a motorcycle, slows down to ask if I am alright. "Yes, I am fine; Thanks," I respond. He smiles and leaves. I imagine this may look odd . . . sitting on the hood of the car just listening to music through my headphones, just taking in the scenery in the middle of a Tuesday afternoon. I fleetingly think back to the sixties and seventies when I remember this was the norm in the counterculture climate of the San Francisco Bay Area. Only instead of the black Honda, it would have been a painted school bus.

I look up and see a hawk flying closer as if he is flying for me. Is this Shiva with his / her magnificent display of wings? Shiva of the mountain top? I have brought a ritual stone, a stone in the shape and color of a tongue from the Tara Pass located at Mount Kalaish in the Himalayas, a very holy spot. I hold it in the palm of my hand and relax into just being with Shiva, the bird. Now the hawk flies closer. Through the headphone, I listen carefully to the subtle inflections in the chanting voice and to the gentle ringing of the bells. I open my fifth chakra, open to receive. A passage of Rumi comes to mind, "Open the window in the center of your chest. And let the spirit fly in and out."[161] I see the ocean fog bank in the distance. On the next exhalation, I begin to chant along with the music. I realize that I can sing loud out here. My larynx constricts; my throat begins to feel sore. I sadly think this must be from lack of singing, sounding, not enough play. I put my hand on my throat. It vibrates like a Tibetan singing bowl. The birds accompany me. I relax completely with the sun warming my skin as I chant to the music to Shiva. Now there are two birds, then three dancing in the sky above me, as if curious or wanting to join me. It occurs to me that this display of the birds as Shiva is the divine numen in the manifestation of form. I decide to join them in the dance in the gentle mantra of sound, *Om Nama Shivaya.* I feel peaceful and very connected in this moment to the surroundings.

When the last note of the mantra sounds, it marks the time that departure is near. I leave Shiva incense in the middle of the road and for the Shiva bird, raise my arms like wings and thank the numen for this teaching and for visiting me in my dreams. Driving home, I ground my energy by chanting, Lam, Vam, Ram, Yam, Ham, Om, Soha as I imagine each chakra filling me up with rooted energy, sexual energy, the energy of the Hara or center, the swelling of the heart, the cool passage of breathe passing in my throat, the light of my third eye and the beam of light releasing from the top of my head. I drive slowly so I can take in the atmosphere of the green hills, passing cows and bulls (bulls are associated with Shiva) on my way back to the borderline and then towards town.

That evening, I put various feathers in a dream catcher that hangs over the bed. The feathers are placed to remind me of Shiva and my ability to fly or expand my awareness to deeper dimensions of experience. I remind myself that an active receptivity allows for a fuller perception and appreciation of the gifts of life. I think about the rasa of delight, the spectrum of sound cadence, the textures of the light and shadows of sound. I am also able to participate in the dance of feelings and subtle movements and shifts in my body, relax into the textures of scent and tastes and bask in the symphonic expression of all the senses combined, a syntheasia. It is the dance of Shiva. I hang a crystal in the middle of the dream catcher to remind myself of the pristine crystal clear awareness that is the true nature of mind.

CHAPTER 6: RECEIVING THE DOLL:
ENGAGING WITH THE MOTHER NUMENA

The Mother Dreams

1-28-95 protection Mother

I am in a dance workshop led by a priestess. Later, when its dark, she moves towards me, holds my hands and informs me, "She is with you right now, the goddess in her many forms is watching over you, guiding and protecting you. She can see the light within you." I ask, "Why me?" She tells me, "It's the way for you—to be embedded with knowledge on deeper levels."

8-13-95 red moon, mother earth

We are all gathered together for the event. I look up and see an eclipsing red moon. Then, as I watch it beat, I feel the earth beat under my feet. My mother tells me, "It's Mother Earth."

8-21-98 doll of the grandmothers

I am in a shaman circle. The hot sun shines on me. Rocks surround us. A shaman gives me a drum with a snake painted on it and I communicate with it. The shaman tells me the snake has felt my energy; it was completely transmitted. I need to move to another area as the sun is so strong on my arm it burns intensely. Then I am given a hand-carved wooden doll made from a dark wood. She has a doll-like face and a pregnant belly. I put my hands on her belly and look into her face and find myself looking into the faces of my ancient grandmothers. I feel a sublime sense of peace while I am told my mission is one of understanding the wisdom of the grandmothers. I am enveloped into an aura of midnight blue. I am told this is mother Mary, pregnant. The people around me—a couple of shaman women smile.

Amplification on the Mother Numena

I begin with the research I have collected on the *matrioshka* nesting dolls of the Slavs. She is the egg-shaped peasant mother doll wearing a *babushka* (colorful scarf) tied under her chin. When twisted and opened at the waist, a smaller identical doll can be found inside, and when opened again, yet another. She is the one and the all.[162] Joanna Hubbs describes the symbolism of her vivid colorful clothing, "Her red, yellow, blue, and green garments suggest colors of blood, sunlight, ripe wheat, sky, water, flowers, and luxuriant plants.[163] The matrioshka is a symbol of Mother Russia whose land was personified as a mother that provided everything to everyone. Her rivers were called "little mothers" with the grandest of them all, the "Mother Volga." (I am reminded of my paternal grandmother, Maryana Narevska, who perhaps was named after the River Narev in Poland).

Personal mythic material that relates to the mother numena in my dreams begins to take shape in the summer of 2002 during my ethnographic expedition to Russia. After a twelve hour train ride, our research team was greeted the following morning by an entourage of women, a folk dance troupe, dressed in traditional white dresses with predominately red, white and black chevroned and meandered embroidered designs.[164] Most of the women wore elaborate beaded and coined headdresses, some horned. Camera crews awaited our arrival and as we stepped off the train. Then celebratory music and dancing began. An old Baba with her babuska tied under her chin caught my eye. She was holding a basket of hot, freshly baked piroshkis covered with an embroidered ritual cloth and offered one to me along with some warm beer. I gratefully accepted this unexpected gift. Then, she smiled and kissed me on the lips.[165]

The women's faces reflected their strength, perseverance, independence and agency. It was clearly evident in their proud stance and facial expressions, their boisterous voices and body language. Here, men did not dare cross a woman. A solidarity was clearly noticeable among the women, a strong sisterly bond. It was not unusual to see women walking holding hands or arm in arm. When I looked into the faces of the grandmotherly women, I saw reflected back my own grandmother, her warmth and welcoming smile, as well as my mother and two sisters. What was most astonishing and quite startling at times, was a particular group of women (from the west of Chuvashia but no one could tell me exactly where) who looked like they could also be my sisters. I found I bore an uncanny resemblance to them—same hair, cheekbones, almond-shaped eyes, facial features and bone structure, even the same carriage and walk.

On one occasion, an identical twin sister was waiting for a bus. I was outside of a restaurant speaking to a few Russian young people. As I spoke, my eyes and the eyes of my twin locked. Transfixed, we studied each other, smiling in acknowledgment of the remarkable mirror image until she was out of sight, her stare from the bus window moving gradually out of sight. Perhaps she really is a relative, I wondered.[166] Though many of the women and girls appeared Turkic, there were others with Asian / East European features. My ancestry through my great-grandmother line is Russian and grandmothers were from Lithuania and Poland. I later learned a group from Chuvashia migrated to Lithuania. It became quite evident why I needed to travel to this particular area in Russia.

The music of the Chuvash sounded to me like a cross between a polka and a Tibetan folk song. Enamored with Tibetan and Central Asian cultures, the music touched me deeply. I was delighted to be in Russia with mothers and sisters dancing and singing songs that likely originated back to ancient times. They motioned to me to dance in the middle of the circle and as I did the sun shone down on me. I danced to the women clapping the beat. Somehow, it all seemed so familiar.

Ancient folk motifs are still reflected in the patterns in the Chuvash clothing—the zig zags around the hemlines and necklines denoting wolves' teeth for protection,[167] the red embroidered figures of women holding hands or arms upraised, holding birds or flowers, and elaborate beaded and coined horned headdresses. Depicted on the garments of the women's clothing are apotropaic symbols of protection from the elements, from invisible malefic forces of nature, and ritualistic spells. And, there are motifs to confer blessings, healings, and fertility, and symbols to help one "cross over" to the other shore, to the life beyond after death.

Embroidering was not considered a craft; it was referred to as "writing" or "painting."[168] Creating embroidery was handed down by mother to daughter laying testament to a visual text that (barely) kept the sacred traditions and memories of female agency alive. So, indeed, this oral language had a long and ancient history and I was there to witness it, feeling a link to the past. In the pit of my stomach, I felt the despair of the Babas, the women whose contributions have been exploited, undervalued, and whose legacy of weaving story patterns, codifying a world view depicting a harmonic relationship with the environment is now on the brink of extinction. I began to think of the film title, "Shadows of Forgotten Ancestors." Even history books in the West continue to ignore East European history and customs when discussing European cultures.

Much of the trip was difficult. I was in an atmosphere in what I believed to be my ethnic roots, in a pagan environment. It reminded me of childhood memories of visiting my grandmother who had a chicken coup, a cow, and an old barn that smelled of hay and chewing tobacco. I hadn't realized until then how much I missed her. I saw her in the old women, in their strong countenance and exuberance, and in the lines etched on their faces and hands. While in Russia, I learned my long-time mentor, Ani Mander, a passionate feminist who was like an older sister / mother to me for nearly a decade, passed away. And, as I longed for my grandmother, I felt deep sorrow about Ani crossing over. The sadness was expressed as physical discomfort—a weakening in my muscles and life force. I wondered if I had contracted chronic fatigue syndrome. For the remainder of the time while in Russia I reminded myself to be extra-attentive to any over-exertion.

"Mother Volga" is the endearment used by the Slavs and Chuvash to refer to the Volga River. The apartment where I stayed was situated on her banks so that while gazing out the bedroom window, I could relax my mind and body. Two cherished moments of my visit to the Mother Volga region particularly stand out—one an overnight stay at a Baba's house where I was able to take part in a *banya* (sauna, bathhouse ritual) with the Russian woman; and the other is when I prepared to meet four Chuvash women to interview them on women's customs, spirituality and rituals.

After hours of riding on a barely drivable dirt road full of ditches and potholes, a road where in the fields on both sides wolves used to roam and the country folk had to wield torches to keep them at bay, I arrived at a village that consisted of a single row of old well-kept, log cabins. I was invited to spend the night at Dr. Nina's' childhood home and take part in a banya.

In the Slavic lands, spaces considered thresholds of the liminal are: 1) the oven, 2) underneath the home, 3) the attic, and 4) the bathhouse or banya. The banya is located on the edge of the homestead, on the boundary between the homestead and its outskirts, and as Phillipa Rappoport points out "it is filled with steam—neither air nor water." The bathhouse is also a place where 'the dead' congregate.[169]

Any man in the vicinity knew to stay clear away from us women while we took our banya. Beer was consumed in the sauna, branches of freshly cut bay leaves were thrashed on our naked bodies so the oils would seep into, soften and scent our skin. Then, cold water from a bucket was thrown on us outside under the brightly starry and moon-lit sky. The bathhouse was a woman's space. It was the locus where women secretly worshipped in ritual a domestic form of 'bereginy' called *rozhanitsy* and a place where fire and water met, symbolizing "both purification and generation." The banya was the temple for magical cures, prophecy, and marriage rituals.[170]

Pervasive in the kitchen's walls was the scent of fresh baked bread, pickling herbs and spices, fresh greens from the garden and a slight musty odor as if it were layered from generations. As I looked out the window, I saw the Baba looking back at me. This was her domain and she knew it well. Exhausted from the eventful day, I retired to my bed located directly across from the hearth where the old white beehive-shaped *pech'* (oven) warmed and nestled me in the arms of the invisible grandmothers and the ancient Babas who inhabited the atmosphere.

Poles called "Moist Mother Earth," *Matka Ziemia*. Other names for her were *Zaleta, Jezy-Baba*, and *Baba-Jedza*. Many of these names derive from places high up in the mountains, holy places where it is said the gods lived. She was the Golden Woman, the Slavic *Zlota Baba* also called the goddess *Zhywa* (*Zywa*) or *Zhywie* (*Zywie*), *Zhiva*. Her sacred day was Friday.[171] She was the goddess of the mountain (like her counterpart the Hindu or Dravidian Shiva).[172] This is curious. Could the Polish Zhiva and the god Shiva be connected? Was the female Shiva once the all encompassing Mother Goddess of the Mountains? Is Zhiva the same shakti of Shiva in the *Adhanarishvara* figure?[173]

In Lithuania, the all-pervasive Mother was named *Matka Syra Ziemia*. She was also addressed as "the Mother of Plants;" "she who raises flowers." Honored at planting and harvest times, she was the source, the mother of all, the judge. People used to touch the earth as witness to her while making oaths. The Earth was a supreme being, sentient and just; swearing an oath was always made binding by touching the ground, the mother.[174] The following ritual was a part of a Slavic harvest festival,

> In some regions, in August, she was invoked protectively facing East, West, South and North with libations of hemp oil. She could prophesize, if one could understand her. The oath in her name was binding and incontestable. As late as this century, Russian peasant women performed a rite to her to ward of plague, nine virgins and the widows, clad only in their shifts, would plough a furrow round the village, shrieking. Any man who met them was struck down mercilessly.[175]

A rendition of this custom continues to this day as recounted to me during my interview with the four Chuvash women. Women still meet at night and during particular rituals, wear white shifts, let down their hair and stand at the boundary places at the edges of town.

An interesting occurrence took place before my interview with the Russian women. While awaiting their arrival in what seemed like a matter of minutes, the wind began to it began to howl and blew open many of the windows. Then it began to rain in torrents. I took this to mean these powerful women were on their way. I was prepared for them. Arranged on the embroidered kitchen tablecloth were a variety of breads, cheeses, the traditional small bowl of salt, and a bottle of cherry wine. When they arrived, they presented me with a box of fine Russian chocolates. Then, "Zhena," the principal director of the "Uyav" Folk Group, a women's folkdance ensemble and professor at Chuvash Pedagogical University, ceremoniously crowned me with a multi-stranded silver headpiece that she had made while the others exuberantly cheered on. I felt I had been initiated by the Amazons.

Returning to the doll, I researched doll / mother stories from Phillipa Rappoport's dissertation, *Doll Folklore of the East Slavs*. Rappoport documents fifteen doll folktales, stories of initiation where worldviews are transmitted by female elders of the community to pass on traditions of Russian, Ukraine, Belorussian, and Polish descent. Dolls, explain the women, come to the aid of the heroine for advice, comfort or assistance often opening up the earth for passage to the underworld, or "other world" for escape. The heroine sometimes confronts Baba Yaga (the witch or wise grandmother) who lives at the edge of the village and is known for her magic and shapeshifting abilities.[176] Phillipa Rappoport explains,

> The heroine's magic doll is a Slavic variant of the 'fairy godmother.' She is a talismanic incarnation of the heroine's dead mother. The doll also embodies the 'fairy' or sacred aspects of ancient Slavic earth goddess-spirits by acting as a guide in the crossing between the perceived worlds of the living and the dead . . . .With the introduction of Orthodox Christianity in the tenth century, the use of dolls as votive objects literally went underground in the East Slavic lands, while the image of the female helper transformed and came to be represented instead from within the gilded frames of Christian icons . . . . Dolls are still used in villages in south-central Siberia for purposes of protection and healing.[177] The dolls are invoked in order to help with the 'female chores' such as sewing, spinning or cooking, and to act as a messenger or guide between this world and the land of the dead . . . .[178] The 'other world' in the tales means the underworld . . . the world in which the souls of the dead and other spirits reside. It implies an ability to use a type of 'sixth sense' or extra-physical ability, by which one communicates with spirits and beings which are not fully human or of this world . . . but hover on the boundary

between the tangible and the intangible, the conscious and the unconscious, the past and present.[179]

"Cinderella in Tibet" by Wayne Schlepp,[180] tells of a story with a similar theme to the Vasalisa story, and the "buried mother doll" folklore. In Chapter 11 of the "Vetalapancavimsati," or "The Twenty-five Stories of the Magic Corpse,"[181] folktales of the people of Central Asia preserved in Tibetan literature (some claim it to date from Indian Buddhist times, brought by Atisa in 1042 A.D. to Tibet) may relate to the origins of the Cinderella type story. Summary of doll's characteristics include her role as guide: 1) she listens to the heroine's concerns and comforts her, helps her 'cross over' by providing an escape route, 2) she protects her against danger, death, and incestuous marriage; and 3) she stands in for the mother for the daughter when departed to the "other world."[182] The doll is an object which has spiritual, cultural and probably emotional associations with the ancient deities and spirit—from the goddesses to the spirits— connected by their affinity with the earth, fertility, women and women's work, the clean and unclean forces.

Engagement with the Mother Numena

Ritual to Move: 6-14-03

Unexpectedly David and I are informed we have to move from our home on 111 Post Street in Petaluma, California, a city known for the invention of the egg incubator. I used to delight in the symbolism, the three ones of house number 111 reminded me of the triple goddess and often I would imagine the three flowering plum trees in our front yard as guardian goddesses. The word "Post" recalled for me the "tree of life." For six years, our home was like a sanctuary for us surrounded by roses, lilies, irises, apple and peach trees—all plants sacred to the Mother. We even found buried rocks of clear and amethyst quartz crystals while gardening. But, now we had to move.

I remembered the work of Philippa Rappoport and decided to invoke the assistance of the Mother to aid us in our search. As I learned from the work of Hubbs, Rappoport, and from conversations with women on Russian folklore, I knew the matrioska doll was connected to the Mother and ancient grandmothers. She is generally kept hidden and only brought out when in need where upon she is fed and called upon for assistance. In some doll folktales she must be fed in order to come to life.[183] In others she must be dressed first, spoken to and placed in specific areas such as the corners of a room or in a circle around the heroine.[184] The doll as helper performs magical feats opening the earth sometimes to the sound of thunder.[185] I place Tara and the dolls facing the outside world. The three dolls are placed in the north, south and western corners of the house, the east is traditionally called 'the red corner' and in this location I place Tara. I offer her and each one the matrioskas a silver-foiled wrapped chocolate candy and the reddest rose petals from the reddest rose bush every day for a week. I appeal for their help in finding us a new home.

After weeks of searching, a place comes up for rent—21 Raymond Heights. Twenty one is linked to the triple goddess.[186] "Ray-mond" means sun mountain. I consider this an auspicious sign.[187] I happen to go to a thrift store in the neighborhood and find a small clay figurine of a dark mother with two children on her back. Even though she is not pregnant as the doll in my dream, I wonder, could this be the doll that is given to me in a serendipitous fashion by the spirit mothers? I also find a desk light (to help light the path, find the way), and a blue rabbit's foot (for good luck). I bring them home and place them at the altar in the east corner. Soon after, the place is ours. The first to enter the house is the clay mother / children figurine. She will be the house icon. She is placed over the threshold then on to the mantle over the fireplace, the hearth.

The old Russian tale "Vasalisa" is about the realization that most things are not as they seem. The Vasalisa story is told in Russia, Romania, Yugoslavia, Poland, and throughout all the Baltic countries including Lithuania. Sometimes it is called "The Doll" or "Vasilisa, the Wise."

"Wassilissa the Wise . . . carries ages-old psychic mapping about induction into the underworld of the wild female God. It is about infusing human women with Wild Women's primary instinctual power, intuition."[188]

In the second dream, "red moon, mother earth," I am fascinated with the red moon. My research reveals that during a lunar eclipse, the moon turns red, unknown to me previously. A connection to a mysterious bit of knowledge discovered in a dream.

CHAPTER 7: CIRCLE OF MATRIKAS:
ENGAGING WITH SKYWOMEN

<u>Skywomen Dreams</u>

3-26-94 flying at the water's edge

It is dusk in a native island town. There is a celebration at the beach, and everyone is in a festive mood. People are getting their lanterns to take with them on their air balloons or homemade flying machines. I am with a woman. We close our eyes as we stand side by side and enter into a trance. Soon, I can feel the air changing as I breath. We begin to rise. Soon, we are up quite high. I am exhilarated but fear if I open my eyes, it will affect the trance and then we may crash down. I touch her shoulder for connection. As soon as the woman senses my trepidation, we slowly descend and our feet lightly touch the ground. I open my eyes and watch as people float in their balloons with their lanterns. In a distance to the right further down the beach, I can see two people are making an image of an ancient bird woman in white which reminds me of the winged Nike of Samothrace . . . glowing, about to take flight, and a Pre-Columbian golden tumi[189] is levitating next to the bird woman. Both are magnificent, glowing, as everyone watches them ascend in awe. As they descend into the horizon, the bird woman turns into a six pointed star that glows once more, then disappears.

1-1-03 bird women

My female friend and I are going to put on some kind of show with music—women dancing, turning into birds. They look liked birds with their colorful costumes. I go outside to take a break and notice a woman coming up on the ladder. I look down to see a line waiting for the second show. Before the show, the director mentions that the women in there were chosen . . . a questionnaire was sent out to about a hundred and fifty women and we were the ones chosen. There is a lot of drumming and sounds made by the woman as they dance up into another space and turn into bird women—waist down brilliantly colorful feathered birds. Many black women are in the room. Some sacred men also go up into the space.

8-5-03 hawk woman

It is dusk. I step outside from the room of people and from the large tiger that I am petting. I look up into the sky and in the distance to the right see a hawk flying. We make contact and it flies closer and closer until it is flying right in front of me looking at me. It shapeshifts into a woman out in a field to the right and beckons me to come over to her. She tells me telepathically that she knows I help people, that I am compassionate and asks if I would like to get a transmission from her right now—a shamanic awakening. "Yes!," I tell her. We hug and she gives me samadhi.[190] *Every cell is awakened and infused with energy and bliss. The energy will enable me to have stronger psychic and healing powers, I am telepathically informed. I go back into the room and Starhawk is there. I tell her my dream and she confirms my awakening. We hug.*

next scene: *I wake up* (in the dream) *and tell two friends about the dream—about how I was in a room with people and a tiger and went outside and saw a hawk . . . .*

Amplification on Skywomen

In dreams of skywomen, I frequently fly with them, dance with them, observe them flying or find myself protectively held in their wings. They have provided a graced access into realms of unfathomable beauty permeated with love. On a few occasions, I have received instruction and initiations from them. In this section I begin with mytho-religious renderings of skywomen as fairies, angels and janae. Then, I continue with descriptions of skywomen as birdwomen, rusalka and dakinis.

fairy, angel and the jana

The butterfly wings of the fairy originates from the classical Greek *psyche*, which means soul or butterfly. Her wand (another version of the rod of power) is usually made

66

of wood, ivory, amber, bone, or metal and is tipped with a glowing star. It is her tool of transformation and with it she can invoke the powers first attributed to the Mother spirit, the Goddess who constantly transformed everything in the universe into something else. She used to be called Heart of Transformations, "from whom all becoming arose."[191]

A fairy was sometimes referred to as a goddess, queen, mother, godmother, a good lady, or one of the fates.[192] In medieval times she was a human woman of ordinary size[193] with supernatural knowledge and powers, often a female guardian spirit of a deified ancestor who watched over children.[194] People used to leave food or drink out for the fairies. During my childhood, I, like many children, would wrap a tooth in a clean white handkerchief to place under my pillow so the fairy would replace it with a shiny dime. Matthew Fox and Rupert Sheldrake in "The Physics of Angels" state:

> To study angels is to shed light on ourselves, especially those aspects of ourselves that have been put down in our secularized civilization, our secularized educational systems, and even our secularized worship system. By secularization I mean anything that sucks the awe out of things.[195]

Whether they admit it or not, almost everyone in the United States believes in angels.[196] Angels act as guardians, assist with intuition, defend, inspire and are involved in prophecy and wisdom.

Priestesses used to wear artificial wings in token of their affiliation with angels. Invocation of to them was the common mode of magic charms, presented in dozens of magic books. It was universally thought that any spirit invoked by name, angel or demon, would be forced to comply with the magician's request.[197]

The Jerusalem temple connected male and female cherubic spirits with the Holy of Holies in which a priestess and priest engaged in sacred union. The angels were dispensers of bliss. In rejection of women's sexual natures, the patriarchal traditions obliterated them replacing them with male angels.

The female ancestral or guardian spirit known as Juno was originally called Jana.[198] Jana was associated with Diana / Artemis, a lunar goddess representing the feminine aspect of Janus, an early Roman god of change and transitions, beginnings, and the guardian of the gate. It was believed that every woman had a *jana or juno*. That was the name of her soul, as *genius* was the name of a man's soul.[199] Roman women used to make offering to their *janae*. Sacred to Juno (Greek Hera, and before her to the Vedic wisdom goddess Saraswati) was the peacock. The eyes of the peacock stood for her all seeing awareness.[200] Malachite was the peacock stone. Its orbicular markings resembled a peacock's tail. Malachite, thus sacred to Juno was her totem and used as an apotropaic device especially when cut in a triangular shape.[201] Feather plumes were used in her Roman temples and other Goddess shrines. Sailors would carry her feathers for protection. Juno's star-shaped emblem identified her as 'Star of the Sea,' a title inherited by the Virgin Mary, along with 'Queen of Heaven.'[202]

Patriarchal society retained the word genius for the idealized male soul, but left out the corresponding word for the female soul. All reference to the jana and juno eventually disappeared from patriarchal society, while the term genius remained and became a tutelary spirit of inspiration.[203]

Birdwomen

The Lithuanian birth goddess Laima has been considered to be responsible for fertility, the fate of the newly-born, and coming to the assistance of women in childbirth. Found artifacts—birds made from flint are believed to have represented the Laima bird. Originally ornithomorphic, she gradually acquired a human shape, then became the protectress not only of the earthly, but also of heavenly life.[204]

Imagery of a winged figure often denotes the spirit taking flight and shamanic ecstasy.[205] Skyborne women (and men) were believed to be privy to the wisdom of the ancestors and the gods. In Neolithic times the female divinity was depicted as a bird, worshiped as a regeneratrix and goddess of transformation and rebirth in temples and house shrines.

The birdwoman was associated with spinning (spinning life or fate). Her chevroned and beaked face appears on Bulgarian loom weights (from 5600 B.C); the number three, the meander, "M" signs and zig zag designs found on spindle whorls are also connected with her. In some instances the birdwoman is portrayed as an owl with human arms spinning.[206]

Shoymanas were connected with the Hungarian word *sholyon* and the Roumanian word *soim* (which means hawk), mythological female beings associated with the goddess Diana and Yana. It is said that *Shoymanas* are connected with heaven, white clouds, rain and cleanliness.[207] Often, during trance, they materialize unusual objects unexplained by modern science and herbal mixtures which they use for healing purposes.

rusalki:

In Baltic and Slavic folklore, particularly in eastern Poland and Lithuania, the *rusalki* were spirits that resided in the waters from fall to spring, returning to the forest or transforming into skywomen from summer to fall. Spring celebrations included women placing wreaths in rivers, fire festivals, and circle dances. The rusalki were believed to be young long-haired women sometimes appearing in human or animal form, in the form of birds, or as mermaids. Only witches would be brave enough to swim with the them. Rusalki are also connected to dew and moisture, with first accounts of them appearing in the 5th to 6th century B.C..

Rusalki are linked to women of the lake who run freely around trees and near water. They represent the untamed woman, the forces of life and death. The rusalki's behavior is reenacted in rituals of an orgiastic nature. They are connected to the Baba Yaga figure as both are dichotomous, bringers of life and death, figures of transformation[208] and they are connected to the *vily*, as well.[209]

69

Beryhynia: This rusalki was also known as *Oranta* from "orant," (a position to invoke protection or blessings). The name Beryhynia comes from the Russian word *berech* meaning bank or to protect) and was "associated with riverbanks, mists and water."[210] Her home was located by oak or birch trees at the banks of rivers, or by lakes. Beryhynia was known to bring water to the fields, fertility, and good luck. One of her names means "hostess who brings mist and covers plants with dew."[211] Western Slavs were also known to worship the goddess Zhiva residing by lakes or riverbanks.[212]

Among the goddesses that had survived from the Neolithic, there was *Kaupuole, or Kupuole*, associated with flora, and fertile fields. The *Rasyte* (recalling rasa) watered the vegetation with silver dew. Thus *Rasyte* assisted her mother *Kaupuole*. Both goddesses took care of the growth of flora. In earliest times before the rise of agriculture, this idea was personified by a dying and resurrecting goddess.[213]

dakini:

In Tibetan Buddhism a dakini is a female sky-walker, a woman who flies (flights of spiritual insight and ecstasy), a female sky-dancer, or sky-goer who does not walk on the ground.[214] She is illustrated in iconography as naked, dancing on a male corpse with a wrathful expression on her face (symbolic of the ego or ignorance) carrying a skull cup of blood or *amrita* in one hand, and in the other a curved knife or a drum. Sometimes she wears a necklace of human skulls and is depicted with a trident leaning on her shoulder. Her hair is long and wild. She is a wisdom being who can appear in both divine and human manifestations, a protector and transmitter of tantric Buddhist teachings and can move through wisdom spaces including dreams. The dakini reveals herself to practitioners in whatever forms deem appropriate. She manifests at unexpected times, as grace-filled visions, often during crucial life's passages. As well as being a protector and teacher of dream yoga, she is known to cause destabilization, to exhibit characteristics of liminality and playfulness. Sometimes she may manifest as wrathful or repulsive in order to challenge one's egoistic perceptions and 'attached' conceptual thinking patterns. As

Janet Gyatso states—"No one in the tantric Buddhist pantheon represents such slipperiness better than the dakini."[215]

Miranda Shaw explains the dakini is different from: 1) the yogini who is female practitioner of yoga or ritual arts, a female being with magical powers or a type of female deity; 2) a female messenger who delivers success in all endeavors, both trans-worldly and mundane, 3) a heroine, a courageous woman who has undertaken the challenges of the Tantric path with its primal psychological explorations and radical departures from the conventional, and 4) a knowledge-holder, a woman who possesses wisdom of magic, ritual, and meditation techniques.[216]

In addition to 'wisdom dakinis,' there are 'activity dakinis' who carry out enlightened deeds for the benefit of all beings. Others called 'mundane dakinis' live in sacred places located in the world and dwell in the physical body as pure essence of the channels, energies, and essences.[217]

The concept of the dakini appears to have been derived from the indigenous cultures of pre-Buddhist Tibet and the Bon religion[218] which had roots in the religion of the ancient Persians (Mithraism)[219] and the indigenous cultures. *Oddiyana* was known as "the land of the dakinis" in what is today northern Pakistan.

As manifestation of Saraswati, the dakini is the incarnation of the Indian goddess of sound, and muse of learning and literature. Saraswati, originally a river goddess in early Hinduism, was acknowledged as a purifying presence. Dakinis may have some bearing on the European tradition of funerary priestesses called *wilas* [vilas] or *valas*, who held meeting in cemeteries"[220]

It is suggested that dynamic aspects of the dakinis may derive from ancient worship of the *yoni* (female sex organ) in indigenous cultures, Hindu Tantricism, and links to Amazon-like tribes of women.[221] Campbell maintains,

If indeed ancient traditions of both Iran and India reached Tibet and influenced the already existent practices of shamanism, then the curious combined aspects of

Indian Tantra, Buddhism and Iranian cults such as Mithraism, provide clues as to how the representations of the female developed."[222]

Sometimes Yeshe Tsogyel, known as 'Queen of the Dakinis,' hid texts condensed "into a single symbol . . . in the earth, a rock, a tree, or water."[223] Usually she placed them in "diamond rocks, in mysterious lakes, and 'unchanging boxes,' places called *ternay* which were protected by *tetsung* (spirits) so they wouldn't be discovered by inappropriate people.[224] Guru Rinpoche and Yeshe Tsogyel hid the *termas* not inside of objects but within their intrinsic nature or "within the 'netlike' fabric of phenomena."[225] Some disciples of Guru Rinpoche hid termas by burying them in the earth. These are called *sater* or "earth treasures." The *gongter* or "mind treasures" are termas received in divine revelation by "birds, trees, all kinds of light, and from heavenly space." There are "fire treasures" called *meter, lungter,* and "air treasures" called *yangter*, sometimes named "again treasures" because they are found and returned (due to an inauspicious time for their revelation) only to be revealed again later, when the time is right.[226] Yeshe Tsogyel was considered by Guru Rinpoche to be the 'perfect vessel to contain the essence of the precious tantric teaching"[227] and "through dreams [she] taught him ritual songs and dances."[228] In hagiographic accounts, Yeshe Tsogyel is one of very few examples of a female portrayed as the subject of her own experience (although details of her experience with sexual yoga with her chosen consort is not elaborated upon). From the story of Yeshe Tsogyel, we understand that the playful erotic nature of the dakini is not separated from the spiritual. She is female in the wild and pure sense; her sexuality is celebrated, not denied, nor condemned.[229]

Buddhist Dzogchen teachings are based on working with the energy of the body, speech, and mind, and *Rigpa*, which is divine intelligence. Dzogchen's series of purification and meditation practices prepares one for a continual state of Rigpa.[230] These teachings are said to have originated in Oddiyana.

72

Vajrayogini (or Vajravarahi) is the red, semi-wrathful female celestial buddha whose pure land is called Dakini Land.[231] In an esoteric form, she is sometimes depicted as sow-headed and is usually represented dancing on a corpse and sun disk. As an important *yidam*, she has her own sadhana which is considered advanced and not recommended for beginning students. She is also connected to the night and dreams. In the Candamaharosana-tantra, Vajrayogini reveals her metaphysical link to women when she repeatedly states that she reveals herself in and through them.[232]

Engagement with Skywomen

Skywomen Ritual: 9-26-03

I had considered drawing the skywomen. The process of sketching and painting recalled for me extended periods of focused attention and immersion into the chosen subject matter. Then, I thought of creating an elaborate ritual in her honor incorporating Authentic Movement practice or a guided meditation to the hawkwoman. Perhaps I could prepare a spirit journey to the upper world using anthropologist's Felicitas Goodman's and Belinda Gore's "ecstatic body postures" based on ancient iconography that facilitates flying with birds, becoming a bird, meeting a bird numen. As enticing as this sounded, it would require construction of a specifically designed slant board of thirty-seven degrees to serve as a kind of "launching pad." So, I decided to save that endeavor for another time.

Finally, to engage with the skywoman's many epiphanies, I began to collect images of a fairies, angels, rusalkis, dakinis, apsaras, and hawkwomen in preparation for a ritual. I would meditate and sit with them on a day after the dark moon, a time of increase. The ritual would mark an opportunity to gather with my circle of personal 'matrikas'[233] who have supported and blessed me over the years. It would allow me a chance to acknowledge the initiations offered to me during the past decade and reciprocate with gratitude and offerings.

I selected one picture of each skywoman then placed them in a circular pattern on an embroidered ritual cloth in front of the fireplace. I picked a fully bloomed fragrant lavender sterling rose from the garden. The rose, an offering would represent joy. Other offerings to the skywomen included: water (rasa), honey (to represent sexuality), a red lit candle (passion), saffron (for women's wisdom), sesame seeds (for growth and abundance), and three peacock feathers (in honor of my *jana*, her lineage, and her all-seeing nature). In my women's space, alone in the house with the matrikas, I sat in the middle space, lit juniper incense, showered myself with the rose petals and entered into meditation. Boundaries thinned, then dissolved. Soon, there was no division between us as we sat in a state of spacious bliss.

CHAPTER 8: CONCLUSION

Part One: Reflections on Immersion and Amplification

Through engagement with dream numena—the Spirit of Sound, the Mother, and the Skywomen in *Clarity dreams, Personal Mythology dreams*, and *Initiation dreams*, I now understand dreams as portals, gifts, and navigational tools for expanding consciousness.

This concluding section is divided into two parts. The first part is essentially the results of the initial steps of the methodological design—how I arrived at the topic, the Immersion Phase (the method I used to identify the numena through the cataloging of dream data) and the Amplification Phase (meeting the numena through contemplation and introspection and through review of mytho-religious research, pertinent travel journal entries, highlights from interviews and conversations with specialists in various fields related to this study). The second part is a discussion on the Engagement Phase of the investigation—reflections on the rituals, enactments and creative expressions—communing with the numena. In the Synthesis, I present what I learned from the study—the highlights of the investigation, and new questions that arose.[234]

Finding the topic proved to be the most difficult phase of the investigation. *Focusing*[235] required that I look within, use a "felt sense" to determine what I wanted to concentrate on. Writing a book requires a commitment to a lengthy, in-depth study. So a primary determinate was that it offer personal and transpersonal possibilities. It had to be a topic that would hold my interest for the duration of the work, as well as offer insight to the readers.

There were many topics I attempted and wanted to include them all—my spiritual and meditative practices, experiences with bodywork and breathwork both as a practitioner and client, pilgrimage tours to sacred sites and the mystical and imaginal realms visited in my dreams. To include everything, however, would create an unwieldy project, as became obvious after a few attempts. I had to narrow it down, figure out what had the most 'juice' for me. To choose one seemed simple enough in theory. On the contrary, I found them all vying for attention. Often I felt caught in the middle of a swirling vortex of ideas, images, getting more confused as where to find an entry point. I had collected an enormous amount of material—so many colorful threads to create a design.

During the early stages of the project, I decided to allow the topic freedom to take a life of its own. The challenging, provocative and innovative approach derived from Organic and Heuristic Inquiries intrigued me. It meant the topic could move, turn, change directions, grow naturally on its own accord. It didn't occur to me that it may want to gestate for a long period of time.

Because of the non-linear, loose structure I designed, I found myself in unknown territory, swimming in an "unknown current."[236] I had a difficult time navigating, staying on course and became impatient and stressed, feeling the desperate need for a compass or map. When I steered toward a more linear direction, it resisted. I yearned for stronger perimeters but knew the work needed time and space to develop.

Faith, trust, and surrender was what this project required and patience which is challenging for me at times. I asked the dream numena for advice. The response was 'from the middle out,' like working with clay to produce a vessel.

I tried 'clustering' (see Chapter 2). By working from the middle out, clustering helped me clarify the range of interests by grouping them. I wrote "juice" in the middle of a large piece of newsprint paper. Among the themes that spidered out were: 1) Tara, the female Buddha, 2) female wisdom beings of Nepal and India, 3) female wisdom beings of the Slavic and Baltic traditions, 4) female shamanic traditions, 5) numinous experiences in Authentic Movement practice, 6) numinous experiences in dreamwork, 7) shapeshifters, 8) the 'guardian of the gate' mythologem, 9) The Jana/ Janus mythologem, 10) mytho-religious symbology in women's folkdress patterns, and 11) numinous presence, in general. I placed imagery around the house to see if one would call out to me more than the others.

One day I happened to pick up a book at a local bookstore, *The Vein of Gold* (1996) by Julia Cameron. Serendipitously, I opened to a passage that immediately piqued my interest, "Walking is the most powerful creative tool that I know . . . [it] replenishes our over-tapped creative well and gives us a sense of . . . wellness."[237] Soon, I began to walk regularly, twenty minutes a day and one hour long walk a week, as suggested. It oxygenated my cells and reviving my 'chi' (life force). It renewed me physically, mentally, as well as provided breaks from concentrated sedentary work. During these walks, I did not bring my portable CD player or listened to lectures or music, as I had been accustomed to. Rather, I walked with the intention of noticing the surroundings, sensitive to what appeared in my immediate field of vision—the birds, flowers, the breezes, the movements of my steps, my joints and muscles limbering. Moving in the fresh air improved the quality of my breath which enhanced my awareness and increased my stamina. It provided for time to just 'be' without thinking.

As part of the organic and heuristic processes, keeping a journal is recommended. Not a journaler (except for the dreams and for fieldwork), I resisted this method of immersion. But, considering this work is of an introspective nature, I decided to go ahead and stream-of-thought journal.

The following are brief excerpts of few reflective journal entries:

7-23-02: *I noticed today during meditation how far I was from the point of calm. Then slowly, gradually, I was able to quiet my thoughts by focusing on my breath. Ham, Sa . . . Ham in breath, and Sa, out breath. I learned this from Rinpoche. This mantra served as a successful device in order to return me back into the present moment.*

1-24-03: *Perhaps a reason I'm attracted to the archetype of the shapeshifter is because she is a mover. She can change realities in an instant. She can be a bird, a deer, a warrior woman, naked and aggressive, her voice is not muffled. She can enter many atmospheres, the past and future, the lower and upper world, the land of Uddiyana[238] where all is peaceful, loving, beautiful. And, she can fly. The shapeshifter represents the integrated woman, in touch with all expansive aspects of herself.*

It is evident now that if I hadn't written down my thoughts to reflect upon a year later, I may not have recalled them and other early musings that contributed to envisioning the path ahead.

Another immersion technique was to read my colleagues' dissertations specifically on topics related to experiences of the numinous. Cautious about becoming too influenced but curious how they designed theirs, I read a few. The work of Tricia Grame,[239] Sharon Williams,[240] Mari Pat Ziolkowski,[241] and Susan Carter[242] particularly interested me. Tricia, an accomplished artist, wrote about her relationship with the Virgin Mary in an autobiographical and artistic rendering of her experiences. Sharon, also an artist, painted her words in an elegant style of reflective writing using imaginal methods in a study about her experiences in the forest. Mary Pat's dissertation, grounded in Rhea White's Extraordinary Human Experiences, illustrated the unbounded voice of the Hindu goddess Kali. Susan used a more traditional, informative, interdisciplinary approach in her pioneering study of the Sun goddess of Japan, Amateratsu.

The following represents a succession of topics that preceded and influenced my decision to focus on numinous dreams.

Tara and the Dakini

Since returning to school to complete my B.A., I had intended to investigate the iconography, and mythology of Tara, the female Buddha of Indian and Tibetan Buddhism, and the Tantric Hindu Tradition, as well as explore the concept of the *dakini* from the perspective of a Western woman on a spiritual path. For several years, both Tara and the dakini provided me with models of highly realized beings in female form— powerful figures with features of embodied spiritual vitality that I found lacking in my early Catholic religious upbringing. I was compelled to travel to India and Nepal, lands where they had been known to manifest. Years later, my Master's thesis *Women, Sakti, and the Goddess: An Investigation on the Veneration of Hindu Female Deities* was to serve as a foundation for further exploration on female Buddhist deities.

Woman as Goddess Adorned

As I continued to study the history, myths and artifacts of the tantric goddesses, in particular Tara and the dakini, I became aware of the need to explore my own roots. This became particularly compelling after hearing lectures by Professor Lucia Birnbaum on the values of researching one's ancestral heritage. I felt an urgency to discover if similar figures to the dakini existed in the pre-Christian cultures of the Slavic / Baltic traditions. So, I embarked upon a study of a symbolic language of the oral traditions of Eastern Europe—embroidery motifs in folk dress in preparation for travel to Russia (2002). In addition to museum research of Slavic iconography and folklore in Moscow, I joined a team of folklore specialists (Mary B. Kelly and Sheila Paine) in an expedition to document the rituals and folk dress of the Volga peoples.[243] I was particularly interested in the 'orant' or upraised arms stance of the female figures displayed in the embroidery patterns, the horned headdress, and women's rituals. My intention for a sub-study was to investigate the sacred female as priestess, oracle, healer, guardian—her supernatural aspects.

Concluding my search for similar deities to Tara and the dakini, I found there were none (with the exception of some characteristics of the Virgin Mary) as profound in the manner of dynamic, transcendent qualities in extant practices. Subsumed in the folklore and mythology of the region, however, remained the concepts and images of the rusalki (female water spirits), the Baba Yaga (grandmother, shapeshifter) and the matrioska (mother doll). Even though I had collected a lot of material on this topic, due to circumstances surrounding the trip, the death of my mentor Ani Mander, and my physical state of health, I set the investigation aside and eventually became less interested in it as the centerpiece of my study.

My two aborted attempts at a topic exhausted me. Soon, I became aware of strange physical sensations. My body began to go through a succession of unsettling energetic changes. What began as slight tingling sensations became snake-like currents of potent

79

explosive energies coursing through my body or I found myself waking up with numb arms, or fingers, or again rushes of energy surging through my limbs and head. I feared I was on the brink of a heart attack or stroke. My symptoms, however, had some similarities to spiritual emergence.[244] When I discovered this, fear was replaced with a sense of wonder and an openness to possible changes taking place. I became more gentle with myself and rode them like waves. Eventually they lessened.

I needed a rest cure then perhaps the right topic would emerge. It needed room to take shape free from distractions, a place of calm to gestate. This is what the spirit of the project requested.

Being guided by a numen that wished to make her presence known was all very familiar. When I planned a pilgrimage to the Durga Festival in Nepal (Durga means the 'ford' as in 'fording' or 'crossing' a river) in 2000, it was Durga herself who beckoned me to midwife the project. For reasons unclear, I intuited I was chosen by her.[245] I had visited there the previous year and also wished to return. For a full year, much of my energy went into the planning of this pilgrimage tour for twelve women. Often I would stand back perplexed and somewhat astounded that I was so driven to create this journey. I also felt confident I could handle holding the space for these women, most of whom (except one) had never traveled to the East. The pilgrimage from the beginning took on a life of its own. In the end, the tour was successful and well worth the work. It was an exercise in surrender, faith, trust, and service to the Mother.

I was faced with the drive to rebuild the momentum for this investigation once again. As it required my full attention, I decided to sequester myself from an active social life and community events. Signals such as synchronistic events and serendipitous happenings began to occur. Many opening of books to exactly the right passages and just the right items falling off shelves vying for my attention. They were indicators I was on the right track.

Guardian of the Gate

The name "Yana" means "the way of" or "vehicle" in Sanskrit. It also signifies the female guardian of the gate, I later learned. "Yana" is another spelling of Jana. Jana (later Juno) is the female of the Jana / Janus guardian of the gate mythologem. The "AH" sound is related to the heart, feelings of unity; it radiates energy, is associated with the earth and a golden color.[246]

After careful examination, I decided to focus on the image of the female guardian of the gate, Yana, the one who stands between worlds.

Shapeshifter

In time, the shapeshifting aspect of the '*janae*' (female guardian spirits) began to fascinate me. Then it occurred to me, I was only concentrating on anthropomorphic forms. Having studied shamanic techniques, I had established a close relationship with my animal power allies. How could I have overlooked the spirit of animals? And the earth, trees, plants, rocks, the flowers that I developed bonds with in my dreams? I became more aware the numena of nature calling to me.

Numinous Presence

My dreams have been vivid for many years. When I discussed them with friends occasionally, they seemed fascinated. Writing about them was a possibility I considered in the past but didn't explore. But now, the timing felt right. First, it was important to get signs from the dreams that I had permission to bring them into the public eye. After receiving positive response, I decided to proceed with the writing about the numinous presence in my dreams. The study would require personal disclosure which made me both nervous and excited. The inquiry would be the 'vessel' or container to hold the 'amrita' or precious essence into the light.

Prior to this work, I gave my dreams some, but not enough attention. After receiving a "big' dream,"[247] I would awaken amazed and grateful, write it down then

81

during the morning read it to my partner then file it away with the others in my dream notebook especially made for me as a gift from David. It was a large white binder with a painting of a dreamer surrounded by flying angels by William Blake and on the back cover, stylized hand lettering, "Sweet Dreams."

Sometimes I would fleetingly think about the dream figures or messages during the day. Occasionally, I would place a picture cut out from a magazine or find a symbolic object to set by my computer or home altar. Or, I would check symbol dictionaries for meanings of the mythologem across cultures. "If only I had more time to devote to them," I would often ponder. "What insights might I discover?"

Here was a topic I could truly engage in. What interested me was that I could entirely focus on my dreams and cultivate relationships with the numena. Never before had I read the entire journal. Over ten years of dreams—neatly typed pages and tattered pieces of paper stapled on to loose leaf paper written in all degrees of legibility—were placed in my dream book. Now it was laid out for me to read like a story. Patterns were clearly evident as well as noticeable recurring guardians, mentoring figures and forces. Re-reading them again, I assigned them individual titles. Reading them a third time, I identified the numena. Counting their occurrences allowed me to realize their frequency of appearances. The numena discovered appeared in the following order. The majority were dreams of interactions with 1) numinous women, 2) encounters with snakes, felines (tigers, leopards, lionesses, lions, cats, kittens, jaguars), 3) birds (hawks, doves, owls, canaries), and 4) plants (iris, lotus).

It was difficult to choose which themes to concentrate on and which to set aside. Initially, I decided on thirty-seven dreams and nine numena, then narrowed it down finally to nine dreams and three numena.[248] The sound, the Mother and the skywoman numena were chosen primarily in response to deep interests to investigate these themes further and my spiritual and mythic connections to them.

The intensity of my dreams continued in frequency as I began to write about them. With increased attention devoted to them, I began to feel like I was living a parallel life.

Now the dreams were put in the forefront instead of the background. The Jana in my dreams spent much of her time learning mudras, sacred dances, mantras, yoga positions. She practiced sounding techniques and other healing methods from teachers, shamans, yogis, yoginis, gurus, Lamas, and Mothers, as well as from animals and sometimes plants. Sometimes she was given transmissions, empowerments, healings. Other times, it was she who was the holy woman, shapeshifter. Often Jana was surrounded by love and experienced ecstatic bliss or union. The atmosphere and geographic locations were in many instances, India, Tibet, or Nepal. Many times, I would awaken with a tremendous feeling of gratitude, bliss and wonder why this was happening to me / her. These feelings would last for days to up to a week afterwards.

My dreams did indeed reflect my interests. In waking life, I continue to meditate and practice healing techniques. I attend rituals with orixas, shamans, yoginis, and receive transmissions and empowerments from Lamas and spiritual masters. However, I am living in the Bay Area, not Nepal, nor India.

Instead of considering this phenomena from a psychological standpoint, I preferred to learn how to interact with the numena, integrate them and their messages into my waking life. It occurred to me the dreams may be signaling me to further explore sound techniques, to connect to the wisdom of my ancient grandmothers and to a lineage of women of wisdom and power. I had many questions. "Were the dreams of skywomen giving me 'permission by initiation and transmissions' to fully embody the magical, powerful, sacred woman in waking life, to merge with the jana in my dreams?" Could I hold that much power? Could I connect with and integrate into my life the healing powers bestowed upon me by my dream messengers?

Part Two: Yana at the Gate: Reflections on Engaging with Dream Numena

Trusting and surrendering to the moment, opening to intuitive signs and softening the heart through Compassionate Knowing while being with the numena was practiced during the process of engagement. Similar to Holotropic Breathwork and Authentic

Movement Practice, I yielded to the numinous presences as they surfaced. This was preceded and succeeded by a ritualistic gesture, acknowledgment, and offerings. Gradually a thinning or erasure of boundaries was noticed and the imaginal was free to be, to express itself unimpeded. I entered into the world of the numena with a purity of intention, fully believing and trusting in their reality. Switching gears from a thinking mode to a 'beginner's mind,' I expanded my awareness to include the intuitive, sensual, telepathic and metaphoric languages. I stood in a middle space, Yana at the gate, as a participant and intimate observer.

Reflections on Engagement with the Sound Numena

During moments in the clarity dreams when the sound numena elevated me to a state of ecstasy, I imagined myself as a hollow flute.[249] Vibrational sound was channeled and worked through me, leaving me mostly stunned but feeling clear, refreshed, heightened, taken beyond the boundaries of waking consciousness. Now, it was time to engage with the spirits of sound to extend my gratitude and be with them if they wished to make their presence known to me in waking consciousness.

In dream number #1 the sound numena appeared as a song / mantra / seed syllable; in dream #2 as a mantra again, and in #3, again I am chanting a mantra as I knelt before the statue of Shiva. This time I remembered the words upon awakening . . .*Om Nama Shivaya*. When I awoke I was surprised to find myself chanting to Shiva as I am a Buddhist. In previous dreams, Shiva appeared in different guises on a few other occasions—once as a shiny tanned nice-looking naked man with long hair and colored powder on his skin walking in the sun. In another dream he presented himself as a man from my meditation sangha spinning while dancing and, in another, as Pashupati at a temple in Nepal.

Through research I learned about Shiva's connection to sound. Since I was chanting to Shiva, *Om Nama Shivaya* in the dream, it made sense to engage with the

84

numinous force by way of sound. I packed my backpack with my CD player and set off for a day reserved for just the two of us.

While chanting the Shiva mantra, I discovered that I had a constricted throat. I needed to sing and sound more.[250] It never occurred to exercise my voice. I was given a glimpse of the transporting quality of the mantra when singing it loudly and the vibratory quality that it produces (I usually recite mantras silently). Since, I have learned more about the dynamics of sound through workshops with Silvia Nakkach, founder of Vox Mundi in the San Francisco Bay Area.

The constricted throat illustrates to me other metaphoric implications, as well. It made me aware that I do not speak of my inner life. It is sacred and if I don't feel heard, I prefer to remain silent. I think this ritual has illuminated that perhaps I need to share more.

Every time I now see a hawk soaring in the sky and there frequently seems to be three flying outside above my back yard, I think of my afternoon with Shiva, a reminder that form and emptiness co-exist, one supporting the other.[251] The moments spent with Shiva felt like intimate moments with a lover. The delicacy of the communication with the hawks in the clear blue sky over a crystal lake transported me to a time that was removed from everyday reality. It was as if I stepped into a dream space. We were able to acknowledge and appreciate each other there on the mountain top.[252]

Reflections on Engagement with the Mother Numena

In the first dream, the priestess informed me that the Mother sees the light within me, that She is watching over me, protecting me. In the second dream, I experience a beating, eclipsed red moon simultaneously feeling the earth beat beneath my feet. This is Mother Earth, my mother informs me. And in the third dream, I receive the doll with the message of my mission to understand the wisdom of the grandmothers. I chose to engage with the doll.

Magical auspicious happenings seemed to occur once I asked for assistance from the Matrioska dolls to help my partner and I find a place to live. I can still see the deep red flower petals at the base of the dolls (and Tara) at their posts around the house, turned outward, poised to watch for the right place to become available. Now I think about the address again, 21 Raymond Heights. 'Triple Goddess of the Sun Mountain.' The Sun goddess who looks ahead, looks back and she who stands in the middle at the gate. There are many messages there for me to explore further. Who is this sun goddess? . . . the Polish sun goddess Zhiva? Folklore tells the Matrioska was once a golden woman.[253] Was she Zhiva mountain goddess?

Receiving the pregnant dark doll led me to an exploration of chthonic doll and mother mythology of the Slavs of my ancestral roots.[254] I was able to locate a fascinating dissertation by Philippa Rappoport on the Matrioska dolls; an essay by Malgorzata Oleszhiewicz "Mother of God: Religion, Gender and Transformation in East Central Europe" on the chthonic mother of Poland who is connected to the golden sun goddess, *Siwa* of the mountains; and the Slavic fairytale, "Vassilisa" and her encounter with Baba Yaga which tells of a girl's initiation into the ways of women's wisdom.[255] This fairy tale led me to discover similar ancient Cinderella-like stories preserved in Tibetan literature documented by Wayne Schlepp.[256]

Knowing my roots matters. I wonder what my life would have been like if I had known about Zhiva the mountain goddess or the matrioska dolls celebrating female wisdom as a child and young adult? Brought up with the image of the loving but passive and submissive Virgin Mary role model comforted me but also inhibited my development as a passionate girl and woman. In retrospect, I see I have been rebelling against this spiritual role model ever since.

Reflections on Engagement with the Skywomen Numena

Reflecting on the section, Communing with the Skywomen: In the first dream, I was transported high into the sky with the help of the skywoman. In the second dream, I watched women transform into birds and ascend, and in the third dream, a hawk woman approached me then initiated me through *samadhi*.

I recall an experience of flying as a hawk in a class I took with Starhawk.[257] She beat the drum and after a while most of us went into trance allowing ourselves to shapeshift. I turned into a hawk flying high over a lush mountainous landscape by the ocean, soaring, feeling the strength of my wings, gliding on the ocean breezes. I was able to ride with the wind. Now in my dreams, I see the hawkwoman has appeared to initiate me into the ways of the shamans. She tells me it is a shamanic awakening that she is offering, which I receive. But, this is not the kind of shamanic awakening I read about. It doesn't include experiences of sudden illness and symbolic dismemberment. I try not to over- analyze it and accept it as a blessed offering and initiation with gratitude and grace. What I do connect with is that I have a special relationship with the hawk.[258] In my research I found the hawk is connected with the *shoymanas* and the moon goddess *Yana*, so this is something to further explore.

In the amplification phase, by writing short descriptions on skywomen of my heritage and connected to my spiritual practices, I was able to discover the skywoman (*vily*, *dakini*) is associated with the *psychopomp*, the one who mediates between the living and the departed, the spiritual midwife who assists the dying cross over. Was receiving the epiphany or 'root metaphor' of the fairy as a young child an early indication that my path is to connect to a lineage of women who assist in 'crossings over?' I did take on this role during my father's dying process. Clearly, one becomes a vehicle or priestess, a mediary between realms. For years after his death, I sat with the dying in the delicately thin boundary spaces at a nearby rehabilitation center / senior's home. Hospice work took on a new significance.

It was difficult to choose which skywoman numena to focus on. So, I decided to include them all. The ritual was set up on the day after the dark moon. I rang the large bronze bell to greet and invite the forces of the skywomen to join me. I sat in the middle of the circle of skywomen on the ritual cloth in front of the fireplace. Placed in front of the me, a picture of a fairy—a girl in butterfly wings. To the left was Simhamuka, the dakini; next to her, an angel, and behind me the hawkwoman. To my right, the rusalki joined me, as well as the apsaras. I sat in the middle and instead of the red and white rose petals as planned, I found a fully bloomed purple sterling rose from the garden and consecrated myself with its petals. During this ritual, I reflected on how I never used to take rituals seriously until I realized, how else are we going to participate with the unseen realms? After I placed myself in the aura of the sublime scent of the sterling rose, I spent a few moments to address each skywoman. As I took in the image, I reflected on her significances to me in dreams. In a ritual gesture, I offered them the saffron, the seeds, and then tasted the water and honey. I sat with the skywomen placing myself in the middle, the initiate, in gratitude of their offerings to me for these many years. As I began to meditate, I opened to their blessings and wisdom. I accepted their love and initiation into the ways of the wise women.

CHAPTER 9: SYNTHESIS

<u>Highlights</u>

There were numerous highlights to this study. The dreams were both gifts and navigational tools. With the assistance of my numena or *janae*, I chartered paths that led to panoramic vistas, discovered puzzle pieces that fit, and patterns that created intricate, detailed designs. New threads found along the way will no doubt lead to further expeditions into the numinous landscapes.

My understanding of dreams was limited at the onset of the investigation. As a woman on a spiritual path in search of a more inclusive method to work with dreams, I sought a way to chart beyond the psychological and use a more trans-human'[259] and spiritual–centered approach.

It was clear there was little in the way of literature dealing with spiritual dreams. Enthusiastic about Dream Yoga, I found only a few Lamas and spiritual masters that taught this method (fortunate for me my teacher Tenzin Wangyal Rinpoche knows this area well).

Thus, I began to formulate my own method to specifically to engage with numinous presences. I went about creating a design that placed, instead of the person in the center, the numena in the middle (in the Immersion and Amplification Phases), then interacted with the numena (in the Engagement Phase). Using this model, I found respectful access through the numinous gates.

In Clarity and Initiation dreams (experiences of sound, and receiving transmissions), I was afforded glimpses into deepened, embodied ways of accessing spiritual teachings. As a psychological tool, the Personal Mythology dreams revealed treasures long buried in the traditions of my roots, resurfaced in particular folktales of the doll and the Baba Yaga figure.

It is clear to me now that since young adulthood I have been fascinated by the inner dimensions of the soul or psyche. Beginning with the childhood experience of imagining myself as the magical fairy, I have continued to be steered towards learning the ways of women of wisdom. Sacred journeys to ancient sites that began in my early twenties to the Greek islands of Santorini and Delos, and to the Peloponese initially sparked my interest to study the topic of the numinous someday. It was clearly a calling I felt it in my bones. In my late twenties, I spent one day mesmerized examining every inch of the ruined temple of the Mayan moon goddess Ixchel (again deeply feeling her energy in my being) on the island of Isla Mujeres (means "island of women") months after Hurricane Gilbert. Then, years later, I participated in a group pilgrimage to oracular sites known for its priestesses in Greece (Delphi, Delos, Crete). Summoned by the goddess Tara,[260] I traveled to northeastern India, known for origins of tantric worship including the Sun Temple at Konarak where guardian *surasundaris* or *yakshis* grace the temple complex and to Jagannath temple at Puri famous for its devadasi dancers. In Nepal I regularly visit the shrines and temples dedicated to Tara, Vajrayogini and Mother goddess Durga and commune with the female and male deities in their many forms; to the Baba's house in a remote area of Russia that led me to follow a thread to an ancient lineage of wise women evident in symbol patterns in their folk dress, their songs and healing methods, practices and rituals including the banya or bathhouse—all of it contributing to the unfolding of a personal mythology.[261]

Learning the ways of the transformative spiritual woman, I have come to clearly realize is my root metaphor. It appears I have always longed to feel and embody this archetype. In the process of recognizing, naming, articulating and validating.[262] I have been able to find a stronger connection to my Tibetan Buddhist and Bon spiritual practices, and folk practices and lore of my Balto / Slavic heritage. I feel I have found my spiritual home of *Uddiyana* in my dreams where skywomen teach mantras and initiate me the ways of the magic and spiritual realization. I like to imagine I am connected to this land of the dakinis through my ancestry, that perhaps my ancient mothers lived there, a long ago East European / Asian connection. Results of a mitochondria DNA analysis prove this is not out of the realm of possibilities as my genetic blood line traces back to the Levant, Central Asia and into India, near Pakistan.

90

Receiving the name Yana was an initiation into the mysteries. I think of the spirit of a woman used to be called the jana. The jana in my dreams, I feel, is my double, my guardian. She is the one who speaks to me through intuitions, feelings, and dreams. I understand now I have been supported by a pantheon of numinous presences. They have always been there to provide me with a wider vision of experience and a sanctuary of love.

Dream numena, I have come to realize are indeed harbingers to an expanded way of knowing, seeing and being. Once held in awe, consulted, delighted in, respected and celebrated for millennia in both the East and West, dream guides were approached in ceremony, preceded with purification baths and rituals. Creations of beautiful objects were offered to them, dress was adorned with embroidered motifs recalling relationships to them, and through dance, the use of sacred substances, play and song under groves of trees and on mountain tops people honored them.[263] It is unfortunate that today numena are mostly dismissed as products of the irrational mind.

If I had chosen to close myself off to the messengers in my dreams by negating them as fantasy, I would have inhibited a vital connection to flow through me, one that continues to feed my soul and awaken my awareness. When I lovingly open to the numena, I recover a living link to my ancestors and guardians who inform, inspire and protect me; to nature and all its abundant, living expressions, and to wells of wisdom. Being with the numena has provided passageways to finding deeper meaning in my life, sensitizing me in ways that expand and refine my capacities for compassion, empathy, joy, and love through direct experience.

Hence, 'to drink the milk of the snow lioness,' I understand more clearly the meaning of being on the path, to be a 'jeweled vessel,' as Lama Tsering Everest reminds. I must come to the lioness with an open heart and open mind. For then, I am able to receive her nourishment, her teachings, and taste the rasa of life's sublime wonders and textures.

You cannot collect the milk of a snow lioness in an ordinary bucket. The milk of a snow lion is really extraordinary because snow lions are very special, kind of mythical and powerful magical beings that don't really exist totally in our world; and yet sometimes occur here. The milk of a snow lioness is very, very sacred. But, even if you could get to a snow lioness, get to her milk, you couldn't keep it in an ordinary bucket. It defies the molecular structure of an ordinary bucket and it would seep right through the metal. So, they say if you want to collect the milk of a snow lioness, you have to have a bucket made of jewels. Then you can collect that kind of precious essence. Its the same with the dharma. If you want to collect the precious essence of the dharma, which can open for you the essence of your own mind and cause the conditions that can benefit you and others, then you really have to come with a pure heart. Not just for yourself but for everyone. And expand your mind and expand your heart in as great a way as you can to collect the milk, that you can taste of it and others can taste of it.[264]

Applications

The method I created and followed working with numinous presence in Spiritually Transformative Dreams through techniques of Immersion, Amplification and Engagement (modified forms of Organic and Heuristic Inquiries) may be used to assist people on paths of personal growth and spiritual transformation. Using the three steps I have illustrated in this study, the dreamer opens to access of a personal mythic path unfolding, one that informs through a trajectory that is not only linear, but beyond the boundaries of a space and time, and meets with inherent transcendent wisdom guides that help him / her charter the territory of the supra-subtle stratums and labyrinthine wells of the psyche and realms of the imaginal. A participation with, and reciprocity or 'giving back' to the numena illuminates the way to furthering deeper relationships with powers of the unseen realms.

The design of this method was to specifically address the numena in my dreams and can be used as a prototype. Each path will be unique as it is dictated by the numena as a co-researcher. This method can be self-guided or used with the assistance of a spiritual guidance counselor or hypnotherapist. Working with numena is consciousness expanding. All ways of knowing are considered valid, not merely assigning the rational / intellectual as the primary measure. When our capacities of learning are extended to include teachings provided in both waking and in dreaming states, we are offered a fuller vista to the many faceted gifts life has to offer us.

APPENDIX A: SELECTED NUMINOUS DREAMS

I have included this corpus of selected numinous dreams as a contribution for further applications in comparative dream studies.

12-13-92 changing seasons

I am standing in front of a vast panoramic scene—trees, mountains, a valley, large fields, a huge sky and lakes. At will, with the flick of my hand, I delight in changing the seasons. With a flick of my hand, bare branches bud leaves. The more I continue, the more leaves appear. With a grand wave of my arm, I take whole sections of the view and brighten them with sunshine. Flicking both hands, the scene turns a summery green. I decide to try something new and make it snow on the summery scene. I can feel the cool snowflakes falling on my face in the warm weather.

next scene: A few friendly people overhear me speak. I am not in control of what I am saying—the voice of an "angel" is speaking through me.

12-22-92 the loving plant

I am in a room with a large plant with many large leaves. When I water it, it responds by gravitating towards me. When I acknowledge its life and begin speaking to it, its leaves move at once to embrace me, to touch my face. Its a little overwhelming—the love that is being offered by this plant. I experiment and continue to watch it move.

12-23-92 butterflies at soap suds lake

The entire lake is filled with soap suds—they start to get in my eyes a little. I find a clearing and swim; the water is warm. I look up at the sky filled with huge monarch butterflies. They know I am there and are flying toward me. I reach up to touch some of them as they fly by.

next scene: I am in a basement of a house repacking two boxes taking all the important things and putting them in one of the boxes. Outside there are a few older

94

women. One of the them beckons me to come out. She informs me of a spa she wants to bring me to and instructs me to get on her back—she will take me there. We pass through a beautiful wilderness—a country side of young trees; the altitude is very high. "We are in Oregon" I am informed telepathically. I am struck by the beauty of it all. I wonder if I may be getting too heavy for her and express my concern, however, she isn't tiring from my weight. We arrive at the spa. The woman leads me to a room with a floor to ceiling picture window where there is a magnificent view of a brilliant colorful luminescent waterfalls over huge rock formations. Names are being called for appointments. I hear my name.

3-26-94 flying at the water's edge

It is dusk in a native island town. There is a celebration at the beach, and everyone is in a festive mood. People are getting their lanterns to take with them on their air balloons or homemade flying machines. I am with a woman. We close our eyes as we stand side by side and enter into a trance. Soon, I can feel the air changing as I breath. We begin to rise and soon, we are up quite high. I am exhilarated but fear if I open my eyes, it will affect the trance and we may crash down. I touch her shoulder for connection. As soon as the woman senses my trepidation, we slowly descend and our feet lightly touch the ground. I open my eyes and watch as people float in their balloons with their lanterns. In a distance to the right further down the beach, I notice two people are making an image of an ancient bird woman in white which reminds me of the winged Nike of Samothrace . . . glowing, about to take flight, and a Pre-Columbian golden tumi is levitating next to the bird woman. Both are magnificent, glowing, as everyone watches them ascend in awe. As they move toward the horizon, the bird woman transforms into a six pointed star that glows once more, then disappears.

4-30-94 mouse into a canary

I am in a wooden canoe with a few people on the shore of a lake ready to embark. Its important to the people to bring a mouse along. I am nervous about it as I feel it will scurry around my feet. I realize I have preconceptions about mice. They aren't actually bad animals, I remind myself. I was just brought up in a culture that thinks they are. Anyway, I still don't want it along, so I pick up the mouse, cup it in my hand, look into its face and say "you're a canary" a few times and it turns into a yellow canary. Then, it perches on my hand.

5-15-94 landing on a cloud

I am in the open country. There are lots of trees and a pond. It's wild and natural. In the distance there is a road along the horizon. Three buses are leaving and I miss the last one. I watch it leave with everyone on it. I am afraid. I don't know what I am going to do because I am out in the wild and have nowhere to stay and think I will get cold. There are three other people left behind, along with myself, I now see, but they don't seem to be as concerned as I am about the wilds. Rather, they are hanging out by the pond, wading and having fun. I am apprehensive about what I am going to do.

next scene: *There is a process of some sort—the others know about it—that I will be going through. They have done this before so it seems natural to them. I don't know anything about the process and am getting a little afraid. I am led through its many levels. [Its hard to describe because it takes place on what seems a different plane; I can't even remember exactly what happened.] There are many processes I go through with the people and I think there is a leader (a man?) but can't remember clearly. During the process I go through changes of feeling afraid and feeling insecure but I also want to go ahead. At the end of it, I slide out of a chute and land on a pink, blue and really beautiful cloud. I am completely ecstatic. I felt so completely overwhelmed by beauty. I am in awe and I feel lucky that I am able to experience this. I am lying ecstatic on this cloud. I take in the exquisite colors and the beauty, absorb it into my being.*

9-11-94 in a bird's wing

I wake up [in my dream] *in a large bird's wing. I am caressing and am being caressed by the large white wing. I relish the moment. It all seems so real.* [When I awake I rest in the afterglow of being lovingly held so completely].

10-9-94 jaguar woman

A wise woman with the face of a jaguar is communicating with me telepathically. She telepathically conveys to me deep secrets and we bond. I am instructed to mark the four corners of her face and do so with my hands. [In a dream group, I discuss this dream, how I am frustrated that I cannot understand what she said specifically. I gestalt with the jaguar woman who tells me she does not speak in words but through all senses, that I received what she communicated.]

10-16-94 spin the beetle

I am in a women's circle. We are chanting at the request of the high priestess. She sounds a different chant to accelerate the spinning of the beetle in the center of the circle until it opens up and something comes up from it. I am told this is a Hindu technique.

11-9-94 reviving a bird

A bird is dying. It is in pieces. I place it in the sun and watch it come alive again. Then it strokes me on my cheek with its colorful feathery wings.

next scene: *I watch the black charred bird in pieces in a jar knowing there is still some life there. Everyone else gives up on it. I watch it until it comes together again and turns into a white bird with white and sky blue wings. It comes over to me and strokes me lovingly on the cheeks.*

12-25-94 heart seed ritual

I follow the people to the lakeside. Each person passes herbs, then seeds, instructing how many to take. I am given some of the herbs and two brown heart-shaped seeds the size of a quarter, as well as a flat one and eat them. Standing by the lake, I see a large wave rolling in, breaking close to me. It is psychedelically illuminated. This is my first ritual with these people. They are nice and protective of me.

1-22-95 in meditation

I'm meditating in front of a wall outside. People wonder what I am doing, so I instruct them. They soon lose patience and give up. Someone helps me up and walks with me, guiding me so I won't run into anything as I am still meditating in total peace, walking, feeling my toe, heel, toe touch the ground, feeling the rhythm in total peace.

next scene: *I am given a glazed blue vessel to put in front of me to use for incense during meditation.*

1-28-95 protection Mother

I am in a dance workshop led by a priestess. Later, when its dark, she moves towards me, holds my hands and informs me, "She is with you right now, the goddess in her many forms is watching over you, guiding and protecting you. She can see the light within you." I ask, "Why me?" She tells me, "Its the way for you—to be embedded with knowledge on deeper levels."

3-20-95 flying dog

I mount a brownish-gold dog and hug it. Then, we fly up into the sky. I am not afraid as long as I hold on to it, completely hug it with my arms and legs, hold on to it like a large egg. It begins to get an erection so I hold on to its penis like a stick shift. We land at Stinson Beach.

6-16-95 dove/ owl

I am in a room with a glass wall. A white dove flies frantically. I shield my face so it won't crash into me. Then, I try to catch it. It flies out the door and turns into a large beautiful white owl with huge eyes and wings spread. It just stays there suspended in mid air looking in at me.

7-20-95 lucky dolphin

I am on a wooden ship (docked). I look to my right and in my hand is a light gray dolphin, a good omen. It communicates to me lovingly.

8-13-95 red moon, Mother earth

We are all gathered together for the event. I look up and see an eclipsing red moon. Then, as I see it beat, I feel the earth beat under my feet. My mother tells me, "Its Mother Earth."

9-21-95 jungle lift

Huge jungle animals are lifting me. First I am lifted high by the trunk of an elephant. Then, a giant gorilla lifts me. I sit on its little finger and am not afraid.

10-17-95 green fairy dance

I am underwater looking at fish and the mysterious depths. I hold my breath and use a flashlight / magnet that is able to keep me on the bottom if I wish. When I shine the light every moving thing slows down or stops. I see a green fairy woman leading an ecstatic dance. I join in and dance with her and the other creatures. Its wonderful, however, I am deeply hurt that no one can see me when they look in my direction. It's as if I am invisible and I just can't understand it as I feel so dynamic and . . . visible.

11-2-95 gift of ocean mist

My two sisters are in the room with me. By my open bedroom window, I look out to watch a giant ocean wave coming towards me. It's beautiful and has a special name, tsunami. I am informed later [in the dream] *the wave had a deep pool in its center. I stand there waiting for the water to come in the window. It may get things wet but I don't care. I want it to partly wash over me. I know it won't hurt me. I want to feel its power. As it comes closer I raise my arms and surrender and feel its mist cleansing me. Its mist is charged by another dimension. I am engulfed in it. I let it absorb into me completely and know it is a gift.* [When I wake up my inner voice tells me that it is a vision gift—a response from my request at the Skotino Cave in Crete, from the Mother.]

12-4-95 dancing mudra man

A sacred man is showing me how to balance myself on one foot. I follow his graceful hand movements in the sacred dance.

12-14-95 baby in hand

I hold in the palm of my hand a newborn baby.

12-16-95 receiving her

Power and knowledge are coming up through the mother of the earth into a priestess / shaman. She transmits it to me and I absorb it. Later I find amulets with colored stones on them and Motherpeace tarot cards.

12-17-95 gifts for the bird woman

I stay in a commune of sorts with a friend and his two male friends who have a touring / fishing business. They catch large fish off the island. During one of the days of my stay, I go into a room where there are three nice looking men. They think I am the most beautiful woman they have seen in a long time. I am topless and feel very alive and beautiful. One handsome man named Ganja hands me a bird mask made of wood and feathers. Another gives me a large silver arm cuff adorned with gems and the last man gives me a carved prayer stick with his shadow on it. They are awestruck when I put on the bird mask.

12-18-95 Jerusalem snake trance

I am traveling with a group of women. In my mind's eye I can see an overview of the place. I see the ancient stone structures and buildings realizing it's Jerusalem. The bus stops at a roadside store and I get off the bus with some of the other women. I notice purses for sale hanging outside of the store. The dark tan leather seems moist like skin. I am fascinated by them. When I look away, in the corner of my eye, I can see a design of the zodiac on one of them but when I looked at it straight on, it disappears. I experiment with this a couple times. The old woman who owns the store seems eager that I may be interested in purchasing it. I go inside. In the back of the store from where I stand, I see snakes appearing in multitudes, all different sizes, colors and shapes. I see a beautiful black with white dotted snake and a small bright green one. These are my favorites. I know I will probably touch one with my feet or legs if I try to move away.

next scene: *I am lying down and see a huge yellow / brown / white snake coming out of the baseboard. It comes straight towards me and I can't see where it ends; it just keeps coming out of the wall. It slithers up the side of my naked body, rests for a moment while I touch its skin, feel its aliveness, the warmth against my hands and face. I stare straight at the textured skin in front my face, examining the patterns, sensing it's not going to hurt me. Still, I won't move and can't anyway as I am deeply in a trance.*

next scene: *I am huddled in a corner with two local men. The snake wraps around me moving slowly. I can feel its head by my inner thighs and feel the flick of its tongue. I am in a trance again. Soon, it comes into me and releases a cool, white liquid. It retreats then repeats the action again. It is gentle and I let go into the experience. I come out of the trance and realize that one of the men might have entered me and feel violated. But*

101

then I see the snake approach my shoe. It can smell my scent on it and wraps itself around and in it until the snake became small enough to fit around, then in the shoe. This is a signal that it was indeed the snake, not the man who entered me. [When I wake up, the air, I notice, is luminous. I am affected by the intensity of the dream for a week].

1-6-96 amber head

A man hands me a life size head-shaped piece of amber. I put it over my head and look through it seeing reflections of ancient insects, etc. It conforms to my face.

2-14-96 Asian American prophet

He is an Asian / American, kind of nice looking with calm eyes. I know he is spiritually awakened. He tells me in 1997, not this year (as I have more to learn), I will be awakened to knowledge and I will teach others a kind of mantra with the voice. He draws his name as a picture and attaches it to his card. I tell him to wait as I search for my card. A large screen is by us so I bring up images telepathically and stop them at will. I am going to make a unique card out of an image of wonderful colorful jungle animals, maybe a gorilla, tiger, etc. Then I realize that the technology won't be able to transfer the image to a card. So, I find a piece of raw papyrus and write my number on it, telling him I live in Marin. He informs me he lives in Sausalito and here we are so far away in Asia.

3-16-96 mermaid

I see a beautiful goddess with white hair swimming underwater in the sea as I look down at ocean floor.

4-28-96 tigers and the gorilla

I am in the forest with a group of women climbing a mountain. We get separated. Two tigers pass me. I lay down and one lays down behind me, against me. I can feel its fur and its breath. I know it won't hurt me as long as I stay still. There is a gorilla in the forest also who is my ally and is looking for me.

5-17-96 mystic lion

I am on my way to see a mystic and walk by two large golden dogs. One comes over to me and I see it's a very large mountain lion. It walks next to me and puts his jaws around my arm. I walk slowly communicating with him through my aura that I am of a higher nature, while I study his powerfully handsome profile. He turns, looks at me and then we study each other faces, taking in the beauty of each other, melting into each other's presence.

5-26-96 beaming

I am standing in a circle of men and woman. A ritual led by a few women, one with a very large silver pentangle ring on her left hand. She is calling for the other powers to come into our circle. We chant. Two purple and turquoise lights appear to the right of us. At one point the lights dance in the circle. A beam goes through me causing a kind of electricity. It also beams at a few other people filling them with its energy.

8-30-96 horned hills

I witness the hills around me turning into the horns of the goddess.

9-18-96 automatic writing

I am led upstairs by a woman artist to her studio (myself, and a few others) so she can show us a painting technique. She tells us a story while we paint. I want to use purple and orange. She tells us an earthquake changed her life. She is from New York City and as she speaks I am hypnotized by the beauty of her words. I fall deeper under her spell. I turn towards the group and have a hard time opening my eyes. I understand what it is like to do automatic writing and find myself following my consciousness writing down a flow of thought that is poetic, coming from a source that is present in my spirit. I am stuck sometimes but then the words flow once again like I am channeling. Then, I paint a picture of my naked body looking down on myself from above. Its very sensual.

9-20-96 snake sled

Many snakes and I are traveling down a couple large hills on a large sled into a wondrous luminous atmosphere of nature.

10-7-96 bird mammal and feathered tiger

I walk outside with my friend. She wants to take a boat to shore where a bus will take her to a bar so she can get a beer. As we begin to walk, I notice two animals which I have never seen before. One looks like a mammal / bird and the other like a large cat—like a tiger, golden and black, but with feathers which makes it look very exotic. I think they may be from Africa and tell my friend not to run or look at it directly in the eyes. As we walk, it follows me and I feel its breathing, its nose in my hand. I am walking slowly trying not to be afraid, then it stings my hand in the middle of my palm.

10-8-96 spider, iris, cat

I see on the floor there is a large colorful, exotic spider. It greets me and I know it won't hurt me. I kneel down and let it crawl on my hand, then arm. Its yellow, red and black.

next scene: *I watch a lone iris open it's petals for me, then close them again. It loves me and I stroke the petals and stem and it strokes my face with its petals. It doesn't want me to leave and dances for me.*

next scene: *I am resting and a large golden cat comes to lie next to me. It crawls all over me, nuzzling its head in my lap, totally embracing me. I don't want to forget the dream [in the dream] and keep repeating to myself, "spider, iris and cat. "I can't find paper to write it on so write it on a gray t-shirt that I am wearing, then on some scrap paper.* [Then, I wake up].

2-6-97 Sekmet's tomb

Down the road I am walking, I see an archaeologist working uncovering a row of tombs. They are egg-shaped and the bone white skeletons are mostly intact, in fetal positions. The one in the middle is larger and the coffin is golden with a head of Sekmet or Hathor on it. I stand on it and am informed it is Sekmet.[265]

4-21-97 dressed to fly

With two other women, I am preparing to fly to the top of the very high tower. We are dressed in goddess gowns that are illuminated. We are going to speak to the large crowd of people below.

8-1-97 the great triangle

A yogini visits me and shows me a great triangle and tells me, "this is a yoni."

next scene: *A Chinese man is driving without any clothes on. Then, he is the passenger and I am the driver, driving to make love. I am speaking wise, oracular words. They are coming through me from a source beyond thought.*

8-11-97 spore and universe

I run into the green field where I pick up a dandelion spored seed puff. Then, I become a spore—the microcosm in the macrocosm. It all seems so clear to me how we are all made up of energy and life, how we are all the same. A tiny spore is the same as the universe. I notice a large moth's cocoon casing lying flat on the field and pick it up. I hold it like a sheet while it blows in the wind. I feel joyous and free.

9-14-97 yogini and prophecies

I notice some large cats walking near me. One is kind of fluffy and black. It almost looks like a dog. In someone's carport, I look under a car and there are a couple of cats—a mother and her kitten. The mother is white and the kitten is grayish and looks like a newborn. I am not to come too close as I am told the mother is very protective. Then, two women approach me. It's as if they appear from the direction of the car (underneath). One is an Indian woman, a sacred yogini who is dressed in a diaphanous gray gauzy sari, head coverings, and shawl. She is chanting while swinging an incense holder of frankincense and myrrh. She is accompanied by an Indian woman translator. The yogini walks over to me and anoints me. She tells me in a hard-to-understand accent that I can be potential royalty, that I may have an early death or can prevent a early death by interference of some kind. I close my eyes while she touches my forehead and blesses me. Her translator wrote many books on spirituality and women. I tell her I would like to go to India and she agrees that I should go.

10-28-97 resting with cats and snakes

In the basement I lay with panthers, leopards, snakes, lions—some sleeping, some awake—all very big, and in one mass. I examine the spots on the leopard as I lay close to it. I try to move slowly so not to disturb them and notice some lions sitting on the steps leading upstairs. A snake allows me to pet it on the head and it, in turn, pets the tip of finger with its fang which stings a little. I am told by an Indian man that the way to leave is to slither on my back undulating my spine, an old kundalini technique.

10-13-97 mudra trance

I sit in a circle of women all advanced in the study of women's spirituality. The teacher instructs me in the art of hand mudras. As I practice, the power of the mudra puts me in a trance.

5-11-98 a holy gift

I visit a holy woman. She holds both my hands and presses her forehead against mine transmitting her energy. Then, she gives me a gift, a large glass pipe partially wrapped up.

8-7-98 snake appointment

In an underground tank, I wait for my turn to sit naked. From the corner of my eye, the large python slowly approaches and wrapped itself around me. I feel unafraid and at peace, ecstatic. Then, it slowly departs when my time is up.

8-17-98 mother of vision

I have my hand on a woman's solar plexus and am working out a big knot. I keep working it out. She tells me I am a healer. She also informs me she is carrying in her pregnant womb a vision of Guadalupe. I lay my head on her stomach. She says, "When I give birth, you will awaken to a new level of consciousness."

8-21-98 doll of the grandmothers

I am in a shaman circle. The hot sun shines on me. Rocks surround us. A shaman gives me a drum with a snake painted on it and I communicate with it. The shaman tells me the snake has felt my energy . . . it was completely transmitted. I need to move to another area as the sun is so strong on my arm it burns intensely. Then I am given a hand-carved wooden doll made from a dark wood. She has a doll-like face and a pregnant belly. I put my hands on her belly and look into her face and find myself looking into the faces of my ancient grandmothers. I feel a sublime sense of peace while I am told my mission is one of understanding the wisdom of the grandmothers. I am enveloped into an aura of midnight blue. I am told this is mother Mary, pregnant. The people around me—a couple of shaman women smile.

9-30-98 flying angels

Two friends and I are angels or goddesses dancing / flying into a classroom. We are all wearing white. I give one friend a red jewelry cloth as a gift. She puts it up to her face admires it; it shines like silk.

10-15-98 throats

I go to a high priestess' house. She is older with shorter hair. As a group of women, we dance for her and when we are called into the inner circle, a few of us dance our dance. I dance with a friend in a free flowing, sensual dance using our arms. Later we dance closer. [I awake to my womb open, responsive, unobstructed like a throat, feeling the sexuality, joyousness how it connects with my throat in my neck, my voice].

1-26-99 spinning man

A man from my sangha translates ancient texts by dancing. It's complex and fast in pace. Then he spins and transforms into a kind of spindle. I feel fortunate to witness it.

3-16-99 magic mudra

A woman rescues me. She shows me a mudra and how to sit in meditative posture. She shows me exactly how to hold my hands to keep me safe from the invaders while I sit in the cave.

7-6-99 kiss of the snake

I am sitting behind a woman who is about to be initiated by the Tibetan shaman. As he goes into a trance, a snake crawls in the air towards her and kisses her on the mouth. Then the snake goes back to the shaman. It feels my energy and comes towards me but as it gets half way, I block the energy as I feel I am not ready. It picks up the message and retreats. After the ceremony, I give the Lama a $5 bill. I am in a place similar to Kathmandu and am happy to know I will be there in a few weeks.

3-1-00 five graces

Five graces fly in. They look ethereal, like angels.

3-13-00 the snake path

There are rock and boulders on the path. As I try to move one, a snake head appears by my hand. I relax my energy so it won't bite me. Soon, there are many snakes around me.

5-7-00 merging

I am asked to read a short passage over the radio waves. I sound each individual word as if it is a song, mantra, or seed syllable and produce a divine-like, other-worldly vibrational tone. I feel transported, ecstatic, as well as somewhat astounded that this sound is coming from me.

5-18-00 light burst

A black shaman man tells me I am well balanced and pounds me on the chest. A bright red light bursts forth from me.

6-1-00 free soul man

Her father is a free soul. He gives me three white pills. I take two of them and chew them. It expands my consciousness. Later, I take the other one. The same man brings me to his workshop and forges a metal bracelet for me.

2-15-00 oracle women

I go to visit a woman who is an oracle. It's snowing outside her house, snow everywhere. Her mentor oracle arrives, a 95 year old woman who looks 50 or 60 with blonde hair, attractive. She puts a flannel nightgown over her clothes to keep warm. She comes over to me, touches my forehead with her hand, then her forehead against mine, and reads my aura. She tells me, "You are beautiful, but oh, a little soft," as she sweetly smiles. "Yes, but I have the power in me," I say and she agrees. We all go into the garage where the large snake is and the dolphin.

10-3-00 trickster leopard

[In Pokhara, Nepal] *In the large attic there are stored large figurines made of wood—tribal goddesses. I notice a leopard or lion walking around. I go into the closet and look through the slats. The leopard sees me, looks in through slats. We are about two feet away from each other making eye contact. I try to convey love, try to connect. Its paw comes through the slats. I am afraid its claw may hurt me but when I hold on to it, it turns into a stuffed animal and I pull it through.*

5-20-01 arms of the mother

[last day of Dalai Lama's Prajnaparamita teachings] *An old woman in India, almost blind, holds her arms out to me. I hold them and know she is 'the Mother.' She transmits loving energy to me through her arms.*

6-5-01 falling with mantra

I am holding on to a structure with two men. It breaks. We are very high up and are going to fall. While falling, I am across from an Asian man and we are both reciting, "Om Mani Padme Hum." I follow his lead. He tells me without words that we may land kind of hard but not to think about it, just continue chanting the mantra as I am doing. He is spinning a tiny prayer wheel. I stay in the moment.

7-24-01 throat work

Marija Gimbutas who becomes Rianne Eisler puts her hand down my throat while working circles on my forehead (third eye) with oil. I feel a bump emerge.

3-2-01 feast of love

[during an intense thunder and lightning storm] *Each Lama / shaman anoints me in his or her own special way with oil. One touches me on top of the head and hugs me. Others pour forth their loving blessings. It is an initiation ceremony for me. I am imbued and saturated with love and joy until I feel I can no longer contain it and feel to the bursting point. I dance with them, kiss them, follow their instructions, bow to the shrine of the Buddha and other deities. The atmosphere is Nepal from ancient times; the air is incensed filled, smoky and shimmery. We are all in altered states.* [I am affected by this dream for almost a week feeling am so charged with energy as if I feel the blood streaming through every vein and capillary in my body. I find it is difficult to maintain a sense of composure while going about my daily business].

2-16-02 horned-headdressed queen

Frustrated waiting for the bus, I walk across the street to where a film producer is doing yard work. I ask him, "Do you know how far away the ritual is?" He offers to show me where the black women are congregating. As we arrive, I see the women are busy preparing for a ceremony that will consist of dancing, drumming, rattling, chanting, singing, going into trance. I smell the incense and notice some of the women are wearing multiple strands of colorful beads on their bare breasts and African printed skirts folded at the waist. I am the only white woman there. The weather is still warm and humid and its getting close to dusk. I look in the distance and see seated above the rest the queen. On her head rests a silver horned headdress etched with faded ancient symbols. Our eyes lock and for an instant we merge. I go into a kind of trance. Others notice this interaction. In a few moments, two priestesses inform me that she wishes to meet with me. I follow them and drop my purse to the ground even though I know it contains $500. They are leading me to the other side, to the purification bathing area so that I may prepare to meet with the queen. I am instructed to sit in the adjacent waiting area. One priestess *informs me, "You are half way there." In moments, I follow her to a bathing room where she pours purified, consecrated water over my hands. Then, together we walk to the shore and swim out to the island where the horned high queen is waiting for me.* [I wake up intent to further research horned headdresses and horned goddesses.]

8-12-02 horned lion

I am driving a motorcycle, then running barefoot up a hill. Snow is on the ground. At a distance, I have eye contact with a horned lion. It is a 'lion of the throat.' My friend (female) alerts me to the danger and we flee. I hide in an adobe building. The lion finds me and I pretend that I am dead. While laying there, I feel the fur and pet the lion. It becomes my helper.

next scene: *A seven year old boy is showing a few of us yoga positions that we have to do three times a day.*

9-16-02 snow leopard

I see a snow leopard in the crevices of some rocks twice.

11-9-02 shamanic body work

A well known Buddhist teacher heals my lower back. He tells me a sound healer friend of mine is a shaman and tells me I am one also. Across the room I walk over to a four month old baby who is wise and we converse. [I wake up to tingling sensations going up and down my legs].

9-15-02 water and earth

I take a bath of purification.

next scene: *A Devi the size of my toe is working on my chakras. Then, I follow a path that diminishes and I slide into the red dirt which I know is part of the process. I allow the red earth to hold me and know the animals or snakes will come. Then, more purifying pools, bathing with Indian children.*

10-9-02 beaded man

I asked his name. He tells me "daimon." He has large dzi beads [magical, medicinal rare beads from Tibet] and tells me they are made from sheep bone. Then, he shows me what he collected on the hunt, the sheep drums and all kinds of brown and white objects.

next scene: I am standing in the bedroom and have on a red shaman's dress. Its a short dress to my knees with feathers and silver coins and a large silver power bead on my neck. My headdress is a red embroidered cap with a long train in back. I am ready to go to the beach. I am going to take a young boy and his light cream colored dog. The dog communicates with me. He tells me that what I am looking for was taken by the cat as he points to a picture of the cat on the refrigerator. When we walked towards the truck he jumps on me and we hug.

10-16-02 bead man, part two

I walk with the black man. He tells me about a naked man in India who wears a dzi bead only.

next scene: In a middle of a circle of black women, I sing a song. My voice is lovely.

11-21-02 deer birth

I am giving birth to a deer but its head, antlers and body are coming into me instead of out of me so that I can embody and become the deer.

12-5-02 standing and sitting meditation

A Chinese master is showing me how to stand properly in a mediation group, a standing meditation. He is showing me a more correct posture. My Lama is glad I am there. It has to do with chi. The master lets me know I have very refined chi. At one point, someone offers me something more comfortable to sit on while I am sitting in meditation posture. There are about twenty people in the room.

12-8-02 butterscotch topaz

I am holding nuggets of golden topaz. I can taste them while I hold them in my hands. They taste like butterscotch. I taste through my pores.

12-26-02 soma experiment

I am laying down. There are present three very nice looking men. I am chosen to have an experiment done. The group I am with already had it done. They hook me up to a type of an electrode. It is the 'soma' experience. I go into an altered state. They instruct me to put some gold on top of my head. It appears these men are from another dimension.

    next scene: I am walking across the street. There is a large unidentifiable animal that is from that same dimension. It comes over to me. I pet it and its claws slightly penetrates my skin.

1-1-03 bird women

My female friend and I are going to put on some kind of show with music . . . women dancing, turning into birds. They look liked birds with their colorful costumes. I go outside to take a break and notice a woman coming up on the ladder. I look down to see a line waiting for the second show. Before the show, the director mentions that the women in there were chosen . . . a questionnaire was sent out to about a hundred and fifty women and we were the ones chosen. There is a lot of drumming and sounds made by the woman as they dance up into another space and turn into bird women . . . waist down brilliantly colorful feathered birds. Many black women are in the room, some sacred men go up into the space, also.

1-16-03 white reindeer

I am in Australia and it's really beautiful. My sister and I have to go down the stairs, many, many stairs. We kept turning the corner, more stairs. Finally, we find a door and go outside. We are walking on a beautiful and spacious island. I ask the black man as he walks by, "Are we in Australia?" He responds, "Yes, we are in Australia." Then to the right I see a very large white reindeer. I can't believe it. I am so happy I have a camera with me. Its large antlers look like icicles. I know I am in the right place when I see the reindeer—that I am destined to be there. Then, I see another one. We go into a building and I retreat to a room with a curtain in the middle. There is a woman who is going to bathe me. I look on the wall. Set in there is coral and silver jewelry in a case, jewelry made in Australia.

1-17-03 the play

I am a little late entering the theater. I sit down with a couple friends, have a good seat and a good view. My ex-husband is going to be in the play. Some people in the audience are given special mantras and tablets to eat for a later designated time. The tablets have something etched on them in Sanskrit. During curtain time (intermission), those chosen recite their mantras and eat the tablets. After I chant then eat mine, I begin to rise up in the air. I keep rising and rising until I am above the clouds. When I look down, everything is so astoundingly beautiful. I am filled with bliss. I am getting a little nervous because I am so high up. I realize its just all in my mind. The fear is just a projection of my mind. Then, I feel fine to enjoy being up there, so high, enjoying this experience.

1-21-03 Shiva's shrine

I am in India and a fatherly man is teaching me. He is telling me that I have a blue aura. He sketches a picture of me sitting in a meditation posture. Then with an azure blue crayon draws in rays of blue to depict my energy field. He tells me, "Yes, your aura is blue."

next scene: *A woman and man teach me Indian dance movements forming mudras with my hands. There are others in the class (held outdoors) practicing mudras as well. I let go. My arms move on their own and take on their own energy; they feel like snakes. I observe this in wonder and curiosity.*

next scene: *The woman and man cut an outfit for me out of a shimmery golden Indian material. Then, the man gives me some clay and shows me how to work with it forming it from the middle out. I can see the person next to me has created some kind of scene with his clay.*

next scene: *I am walking in a temple setting in a place that looks like Kathmandu. An unidentifiable animal in a pear tree comes down and begins to follow me. I am instructed mentally not to make eye contact with it, to ignore it and it will turn around and go away which it does. I walk along the path and come upon Shiva's shrine—a statue of Shiva inside an open temple where there is a place to rest my forehead. I bow down and begin to recite the mantra to Shiva . . . "Om Nama Shivaya." I enter into a deep devotional trance.*

1-25-03 bird camp

I am with a group of women at some kind of camp. At one point I join the others in taking a posture of a bird. Later, we are going to go for a walk. I look down and there are crystals with jewels on them and a pendant. They lay among the rocks as if offerings.

next scene: *I'm at a party. Inside it's summer and outside is winter. In the backyard there is snow on the ground. In another section it's tropical. My friend is about to sing Indian songs while playing her vina. She reads something first and is unsure of the pronunciation of the word Pashupati. She asks me in the audience. I tell her she would probably know better than me. She is reading out of a well worn book and asks if anyone wants to buy it. I tell her, "I might."*

116

2-25-03 crystal singing bowl

My sound healer friend is playing a large crystal singing bowl. We are in a living room with other hippies. Then another man next to him plays a smaller bowl, all for me. I put my head into the larger bowl in order to hear it, drink in the sound.

3-11-03 being the Mother

I am in a room with a holy woman. She is dressed in a sari, sitting in the corner. She asks me, "Would I rather have money or become realized?" I tell her the latter. She shows me how to move my torso in slight movements forward then backwards. She is pleased it comes natural to me. Tears come to my eyes. She puts a veil over my head in a diaphanous material. Only my eyes are showing. A man comes over to pray to me. He thinks I am the Mother. His hands are in a position of prayer as are mine. I step into the role of the Mother, with the holy woman next to me. I am yet not entirely comfortable as it's so new, this feeling, and wonder if I am really ready. I am so pleased, deeply grateful to be able have this experience, however.

3-16-03 spinning urobouros

I set a place for us to lie down and something for our heads to rest on. I arrange it and am ready. When I first approach her I can see how powerful she is. She will transfer images to me. I look to my right three times and see the ocean. The second time I see a beautiful wave. We are on a large boat in India. I hug my a close friend who is there as well and our kundalini energies merge in our pelvic areas.

next scene: A woman gives me a colorful gauze garment that shimmers in the sun. She has one on, too but hers is almost transparent and slightly two toned at the pelvis. She tells me the Devi wants me now. I lay on top of her (Devi) and she begins to transmit images to me at a fast rate. During the trance she tells me my Mars is in Scorpio. It ends with a spinning urobouros. I give her offerings of cloth.

next scene: *I am standing in the center dressed in white, an acknowledgement of my accepting the spinning urobouros.* [When I awake I still feel the Devi's presence flowing through my bloodstream].

3-22-03 lost in tantric India

Walking around in a crowded dusty India, I find out from merchant a cobra is on the loose and she is afraid because she has a baby. I am careful where I walk so as not to incite the cobra. A tour of the inner sanctum—the tantric maithuna begins. I need to go to the bathroom first then get lost. I talk to two women who are trying to sell fashions to a vendor. The material is a nice textured golden beige linen but I don't like the styles. One of the women walks with me. We speak of Marglin, the researcher. Marglin wants to meet with me the next day and I agree. It will be my last day in India. [Frederique Marglin-Apfel is the author of *Wives of the God King*, about the devadasi dancers of Orissa].

4-13-03 dancing mudra man

In the middle of a semi-circle tantrikas dancing. A man and woman dance by themselves instructing us in a kind of serpentine dance. The man then gives us a demonstration of the tantric dance with mudras.

next scene: *I try on a jeweled girdled belt.*

next scene: *I hug a man who is a realized being and he feels wonderful.*

4-17-03 white flower

There is a pure white flower in the middle of the courtyard between two houses. The petals are so white and the pistil is so golden yellow it shines the inside of the flower as a golden light. The beauty of it mesmerizes me. Never have I seen such a spectacular flower, I think. Then, it becomes a large white parrot when I turn around to look at it

118

again. The flower belongs to a woman. I ask if I can take a picture of it but realize I don't have my camera. It is at once a bird and a flower, very pure.

8-5-03 hawk woman

It is dusk. I step outside from the room of people and from the large tiger that I am petting. I look up into the sky and in the distance to the right see a hawk flying. We make contact and it flies closer and closer until it is flying right in front of me looking at me. It shape-shifts into a woman out in a field to the right and beckons me to come over to her. She tells me telepathically that she knows I help people, that I am compassionate and asks if I would like to get a transmission from her right now—a shamanic awakening. "Yes!," I tell her. We hug and she gives me samadhi.[266] *Every cell is awakened and infused with energy and bliss. The energy will enable me to have stronger psychic and healing powers, I am telepathically informed. I go back into the room and Starhawk is there. I tell her my dream and she confirms my awakening. We hug.*

next scene*: I wake up (in the dream) and tell two friends about the dream—about how I was in a room with people and a tiger and went outside and saw a hawk . . . .*

8-12-03 Dalai Lama teachings

I am sitting in a large hall. The Dalai Lama is across from me on a raised platform. He is giving teachings. I am the only one listening. He is looking right at me and I am taking in his words.

APPENDIX B: MISCELLANEOUS MATERIAL

<u>Numinous Influences</u>

Throughout the years I have been inspired by the creative works of the following artists, musicians, authors, and dancers whose work with the liminal, imaginal realms is pertinent to this work on numinous dreams.

David Singer

David Singer is a collage artist well known for the Fillmore poster series for Rock bands of the 1960's and 1970's. His work predominantly contains mystical, archetypal and metaphysical themes such as: winged women, mythic figures and patterns of sacred geometry intrinsic in nature. As a symbolist and independent scholar of cross-cultural mythology and religion, he is also a visionary currently working on a book on an ancient Pre-Columbian ritual.

Silvia Nakkach

An internationally accredited specialist in cross-cultural music-therapy training, Silvia Nakkach has been involved in clinical research in the areas of singing and creative uses of the voice in music therapy for twenty five years. Her extensive body of therapeutic vocal techniques has become landmark in the field of sound healing and music therapy training in Argentina, Brazil, Spain and the United States. She is the founding director of Vox Mundi, an organization devoted to the education, preservation, and performance of multi-ethnic vocal arts. Since 1988 Silvia's pioneering work has been integrated in an innovative curriculum of scientific vocal principles and applications through the Vox Mundi Project programs. Her voice has been referred to as spiritual luminosity.

Anna Kavan

Author Anna Kavan (1930-1960) transports me into the realm of the numinous with her many tales. Her short story, "A Visit" from *Julia and the Bazooka* (ed. Rhys Davies, Alfred A. Knopf, New York, 1975) is one of them. This surrealistic tale is about a woman who wakes up to find a leopard lying next to her in bed. She examines his powerful muscular body, is entranced by his presence. The leopard comes to visit daily. Despite the fact they do not converse, they understand each other. One day he leaves unexpectedly. She sees him once more at a distance. With bittersweet recollections, she cherishes the sublime moments they shared. Each time I read "The Visit" I read it anew. My response is always visceral, a reaction to the breadth and depths of beauty of the inter-species relationship. The leopard and the woman live in a liminal space and time. She speaks to him but he doesn't respond in words. Rather, his actions and eyes speak to her. He represents the numen of the vital primal animal, a creature of a dreamtime space with whom she engages to her incessant curiosity and full delight.

The following are the first two paragraphs of the story:

One hot night a leopard came into my room and lay down on the bed beside me. I was half asleep, and did not realize at first that it was a leopard. I seemed to be dreaming the sound of some large, soft-footed creature padding quietly through the house, the doors of which were wide open because of the intense heat. It was almost too dark to see the lithe, muscular shape coming into my room, treading softly on velvet paws, coming straight to the bed without hesitation, as if perfectly familiar with its position. A light spring, then warm breath on my arm, on my neck and shoulder, as the visitor sniffed me before lying down. It was not until later, when moonlight entering through the window revealed an abstract spotted design, that I recognized the form of an unusually large, handsome leopard stretched out beside me.

His breathing was deep though almost inaudible, he seemed to be sound asleep. I watched the regular contractions and expansions of the deep chest, admired the elegant relaxed body and supple limbs, and was confirmed in my conviction that the leopard is the most beautiful of all wild animals. In this particular specimen I noticed something singularly human about the formation of the skull, which was domed rather than flattened, as is generally the case with the big cats, suggesting the possibility of superior brain development inside. While I observed him, I was all the time breathing his natural odor, a wild primeval small of sunshine, freedom, moon and crushed leaves, combined with the cool freshness of the spotted hide, still damp with the midnight moisture of jungle plants, I found this nonhuman scent, surrounding him like an aura of strangeness, peculiarly attractive and stimulating.[267]

George Quasha

Poet, artist and friend, George Quasha is voyager of liminal spaces. It's as if he is privy to the illogic of the numinous realms, an emissary to inform us (in his poetics of axial time, *oneiropoeia* and other concepts that "uncover") the subtleties that exist in the twilight places before dreams and immediately upon awakening—the boundary places. He mines for jewels in depths of the imaginal not usually excavated.

Here, Quasha speaks of allowing the living dream breath and voice in *Ainu Dreams*:

> Someone needs to boldly go where no storyteller has dared . . . To let dreaming tell itself, to make itself up as it goes, to perform its uncertain limp and inevitable disjunctive leaps—to step out beyond the memorable. 'I can't remember my dream' is perhaps the most common report. But what if memory is only one of the roads in? Or if what one needs is an attractor that calls the dream out into its further life?[268]

Quasha continues to speak about performative listening,

> The torque of telling has a quality of transport, to 'a land' of its own dimension, implying a language specific to another dimension, to which poetry is liminal. The poem is aroused transversely by the listening, is moved to mind the gap . . . The event is a transmission . . . what we are pointing to here is outside the interpretative. Indeed, one protects the delicate life of the dream by preserving it from interpretation, at least until it finds its openness of form, its permission to be through telling . . . The modality here is an expression always of gratitude, a way of thanking them all for their willingness to tell . . . .[269]

Susan Seddon Boulet

Susan Seddon Boulet's (1945-1997) paintings in *Shaman: The Paintings of Susan Seddon Boulet* illustrate numinous presence. She masterfully invites us to view the fluidity of the sacred realms of the upper and lower worlds. We see through her eyes the brilliant displays of color and light, forms and shapes of birdwomen and other spirits as guardians, healers, deliverers. We join her in a dance of witnessing co-emergences, creations. We can almost hear the shaman's song, the drum beat as we penetrate into the realms of the deep recesses of the soul where all living beings draw sustenance. In my bedroom hangs her painting "Eagle Woman," a golden winged woman who reminds me that vistas of magnificent landscapes and dreamscapes are within my reach.

Ruth St. Denis

Ruth St. Denis (1918-1960) renowned dancer, became entranced with Isis (of Egyptian mythology) and Far Eastern deities. She danced her visions of them into expression and considered the dance "a living mantra." St. Denis "recognized that one must first be inspired by a sacred theme or prayer that seemed to live outside oneself, then gradually proceed to embody it." [270]

Lama Tsering Everest

Lama Tsering Everest of the Nyingma school of Buddhism radiates beauty, wisdom and compassion. Lama offers empowerments, teachings in Red Tara practice and Dream Yoga. Her stories illustrate profound spiritual lessons, encouraging the cultivation of a refinement of being.

Monica Sjoo

The late Monica Sjoo, artist and feminist writers was a pathfinder whose Amazon-like presence alone inspired me to keep my flame brightly glowing. Her prolific artwork continues to transport me to numinous realms. While viewing her paintings I often feel as if I am sitting with her in a boat in the middle of a lake observing numena appear. [271] In the vein of Lenora Carrington, Monica offers dream-like images. The Great Goddess, the birdwoman, lunar and solar head-dressed women, the dakini, mother, sister, shapeshifter, and nature spirits are featured in her paintings.

Rasa

B.N. Goswamy offers a description of rasa,

> Rasa means the sap juices of plants, extract, fluid in the physical sense. . . In its secondary sense, rasa signifies the nonmaterial essence of a thing, 'the best or finest part of it' like perfume, which comes from matter but is not so easy to describe or comprehend. In its tertiary sense, rasa denotes taste, flavor, relish related to consuming or handling either the physical object or taking in its nonphysical properties, often yielding pleasure . . . applied to art and aesthetic experience—rasa comes to signify a state of heightened delight, in the sense of ananda, the kind of bliss that can be experienced only by the spirit . . . writers such as Vishwanatha, fourteenth century author of the Sahitya Darpana, a celebrated work on poetics, say: rasa is an experience akin to ultimate reality. . . the idea of rasa came down to us, by Bharata in the Natyashastra . . . placed close to the beginning of the Christian era. But its roots go back still farther for . . . Bharata acknowledges [it] to older masters.[272]

Manmohan Ghosh translates rasa to mean sentiment. Other writers have used the word relish for rasa. A work of art possessing rasa is often described as being *rasavat*, or *rasavant*.[273]

In India, as in many cultures, words for seeing have included within their semantic fields the notion of knowing. Not only is seeing a form of touching, it is a form of knowing. The eye is the truth. In Vedic India the "seers" were called rsis. In their hymns, collected in the Rg Veda, "to see" often means a mystical supernatural beholding or visionary experiencing. There are many ways to cultivate "seeing" in Buddhist practice. Goswamy tells us,

> Bharata speaks of eight sentiments (to which a widely accepted ninth has been added by later writers): Shringara (the erotic), Hasya (the comic), Karuna (the pathetic), Raudra (the furious), Vira (the heroic), Bhayanaka (the terrible), Bibhatsa (the odious), and Adbhuta (the marvelous). The ninth rasa spoken of is

Shanta (the quiescent) . . . even though rasa is defined as one and undivided it is one or the other of these nine rasas through which an aesthetic experience takes place . . . because out of these nine, one sentiment or flavor dominates, a work of art propels a spectator toward, or becomes the occasion for, a *rasa* experience.[274]

Rasa means flavor, beauty and aesthetic emotion according to Ananda K. Coomaraswamy. A person who enjoys rasa is considered a *rasika*. It is a witnessing of pure form unencumbered with elaborations.

The vision of beauty is spontaneous, is just the same sense as the inward light of the lover (*bhakta*). It is a state of grace that cannot be achieved by deliberate effort; though perhaps we can remove hindrances to its manifestation . . . .[275]

Hindu writers say that the capacity to feel beauty (to taste rasa) cannot be acquired by study. And, one's own capacity to be delighted by rasa is the key. Ananda K. Commarswamy comments,

The nature of this experience (Brahmasvadana sahodarah) is discussed by Vishvanatha in the Sahitya Darpana: 'It is pure, indivisible, self-manifested, compounded equally of joy and consciousness, free of admixture with any other perception, the very twin . . . of mystic experience and the very life of it is super sensuous (*lokottara*).'[276]

The Muses are called Rasa in Sanskrit, in which language this word signifies juice in general but more particularly understood as the honeyed juice of flowers; it implies also anything which we particularly delight in.[277] The nine Rasas are represented as beautiful maidens.[278]

Tara

The Goddess Tara exists in many forms and is known by many names. As the Wisdom and Moon Goddess, she represents the transformer, nourisher, the feminine and the unconscious. As the Mother Goddess, she is the expression of the feminine archetype in her benevolent and fierce aspects. In her manifestation as the Earth Goddess, Tara is known to dwell in the wilds among untamed animals. She is also the Goddess of the Underworld as she controls the *nagas, pretas* and guardians of the hell realms.

Neumann states that Tara came into being when the sea of knowledge of which she is the quintessence was churned.

Kumar describes Tara in relation to boat imagery in an excerpt from a myth,

> There is a great hall called *'mana'* whose middle enclosure comprises the nectar-lake. There is no way to go into it save the conveyance of a boat. There is the great *sakti*, Tara by name, who controls the gate. There are many attendants of Tara who are dark like the blue lotus and are sporting in the waters of the lake with thousands of boats of jewels. They come to this shore and go back to the other shore. There are millions of boat-women under Tara who are in the prime of youth. They dance and sing the most sacred fame of the goddess. Some hold oars and others conches in their hands. They are drinking the nectar-water (of the lake) and going hither and thither on hundreds of boats. Of these saktis who guide the boats and have dark colour the chief one is Tara, the mother who can calm the floods . . . Thus Tara, the mother, surrounded the various boats and herself occupying a large boat shines exceedingly.[279]

Green Tara: Also known as Drolma (Tibetan), Green Tara embodies the compassionate activity of all the Buddhas (her name means "the liberator" or "one who saves"). She is one of the earliest forms of Tara[280] pictured with one face, two arms and a green-colored body. Her right hand is outstretched in the mudra (sacred gesture) of generosity. Bokar Rinpoche tells us, "the stems of the lotuses she holds with her hands indicate that all the qualities of realization have fully bloomed within her."[281] Green Tara sits with her right leg slightly extended as if to suggest she is ready to come to one's aid. In her form as Green Tara, she symbolizes the wisdom of all-encompassing action. "She is the great protector . . . who dwells in the forest, the joyful beauty who roams free, arrayed in precious silks, pearls, and coral, drawing beings to her through her infinite compassion like bees to the hive."[282] She will answer the call of even those who don't believe in her. Tara's mantras are: OM TARE TUTARE TURE SVAHA!, or shorter version, in case of an emergency—when time is of the essence: OM TARE TAM SVAHA![283] She clears obstacles from paths and is quick to act, known as the rescuer.

White Tara: is almost always portrayed as seven-eyed, seated, dressed and crowned like a Bodhisattva. Her right hand is in the "boon-giving" mudra and left hand in the "fear not" or "teaching" mudra. She is usually shown with a full blown white lotus at both shoulders; the lotus symbolizing spiritual transformation. The worshipper, like the lotus, grows up through the water toward the light. Tara "work[s] to help sentient beings increase fortunes and prolong their lives."[284] White Tara, also called _Drolkar_ (Tibetan) _or Sitatara_ (Sanskrit), the liberator, is known for her healing powers and compassionate wisdom. Unlike the green form of this deity, she has seven eyes—one in each hand and foot, and a third eye on her forehead to show that she sees and responds to suffering throughout the universe.

Red Tara: "The Lady Twilight was seen, devoted to the stars and clad in red sky, as a Buddhist nun is devoted to Tara and clad in red garments."[285] Although there are instances that the two armed Kurukulla, the fierce form of Tara of Tibetan Buddhism is depicted as white in color,[286] she is mostly portrayed red, dancing on a demon, wearing a mala of skulls, holding a bow and arrow (made of flowers), and known to be able to subdue and destroy evil spirits and enemies.

Black (or Blue) Tara: Black Tara, also called Brikuti, is really dark blue-black but often this color is described as black in the texts. In fact, most of the fierce deities are this color, with the exception of the red ones. Black can represent the "mystery" or emptiness, the complete overcoming of ignorance; the false perception of reality, the illusion of dualism, of anything existing separately."[287]

Yellow Tara: _Mahamayuri_, as she is known in Nepal, is yellow in color, and in her right hand she holds a peacock feather. In this aspect, Tara is considered queen of magic arts, chief protectress and is worshiped for life longevity.[288]

127

Apsaras

Apsaras in Sanskrit means "from the water." The original sense of the word according to Coomaraswamy is *apsu-rasa*, "essence of the water." [289] The term apsaras generally means water nymphs but more often refers to celestial dancers. They were believed to be lesser goddesses renowned for their beauty and danced for the higher gods, as *gandharvas* played their instruments. These heavenly maidens were inspirations for love and possessed extraordinary seductive powers.

The civilization of ancient Khmer, heavily influenced by Indian culture, is known for its temples or palaces of the gods in the human world decorated with apsara carvings. In Cambodia, Angkor Wat's magnificent temples are filled with apsaras in their sensual dancing poses.

Heinrich Zimmer asserts,

Apsaras are the perfect dispensers of sensual delight and amorous bliss on a divine scale, and in sheer celestial harmony. They are the embodiments of a strictly supra-earthly quality of sensual love, Divine Love as distinct from, and opposed to Earthly Love . . . Apsaras represent the "Innocence of Nature," Delight Without Tears, Sensual Consummation Without Remorse, Without Doubts or Subsequent Misgivings." They are the initiating priestesses of the ever-new ancient mystery of the mutual attractiveness of the sexes. [290]

Zimmer continues to inform us that it is believed apsaras wrap "the deceased in their voluptuous arms, carrying the fortunate soul in ecstasy to paradise." [291]

Artwork depicting flying apsaras (*feitian*) as in Yuangang, Longmen and Dunhung Grottos in China is thought to have come from India.

In Indian mythology *Feitian* is said to be the goddess of clouds and water, inhabiting lakes and marshes, and flying pleasantly and freely below bodhi trees. She is also said to be the lover of a God named *Jiletian*. In Buddhist scripture, Feitian is called the goddess of heaven song or music, who can play music and sing songs. Moreover, being fragrant, she is also referred to as 'Fragrant goddess with sweet voice'. . . [She is always portrayed as a young girl] . . .Slim in figure, plump in face, unstrained in manner and gentle in mood. What deserves our attention

128

most is that Feitian in Dunhuang is bare without wings and feather. A ribbon fluttering elegantly and beautifully, Feitian displays a moving scene that a group of girls are flying and dancing freely in the sky. Some girls are going through clouds and rivers, fruits in hand; Some are playing moving and beautiful music.[292]

On Pilgrimage

Carol Christ explains the term pilgrimage, "Pilgrimage, in Jungian terms, is an expression of, and an effort to circumambulate the Self, to 'quicken the divinity' by bringing the Self within us to life."[293]

Jean Shinoda Bolen, author of *Crossing to Avalon* describes motivations for going on a pilgrimage,

> Pilgrims go to sacred places to experience a kind of numinosity or to be purified, to receive a blessing, or to become healed. They are looking for new experiences in travel, with deeper meaning, something to happen within themselves. When a woman embarks on a pilgrimage, she leaves everyday roles at home. This enables a freeing of expression for other sides of her personality to surface. As day to day structure gets broken down, she gives herself permission to vehicle into the depths of her being, where creativity and sources of spirituality live, and where 'spirit' speaks to her. She allows herself the joy of a new vision and even to experience the pain that gives it birth.[294]

Dr. Bolen shares with us a moment of reflection from her pilgrimage to Glastonbury:

> On the pilgrimage, I went to sacred sites and absorbed the invisible nourishment that I sensed was there. It was soul food. Mother's milk to nourish the divinity within the pilgrim. I found that I was not taking things in primarily with my eyes and mind anymore. I was instead feeling my way, perceiving the energies . . . with my body, . . . I felt myself acting like a tuning fork or dowsing rod . . . .[295]

Threes, and the triangle

Chanting three times, or repeating a phrase three times is often associated with an intention to make something whole or to make an event happen, to produce a magical effect, a manifestation or completion—one being not enough, unchallenged, static, and four being superfluous.

In ancient cultures, triangles, triple lines or tri-patterns have been found to reflect people's observation of the power of threes. In Minoan times, shrines and columns were commonly placed in threes and in Turkey, triangular patterns have been found in kilim patterns going back, likely, to the patterns found in Catal Huyuk. The upright triangle signified the sun, fire, or male principle in many cultures; and the downward pointing triangle represented the female principle or vulva.

When constructing a triangle with a compass, a *vesica pisces* can be rendered. So, it is understandable that in ancient times in celebratory rituals to the goddess, triangular shaped cakes representing the womb of the mother were made in her honor.

The triangle of life is also called the *Kali Yantra*, the meditation sign of the vulva. The point in the middle that connects the two triangles is referred to as the *bindu* in Tantric Yoga. Gypsies whose religious and racial roots originated in India used the downward pointing triangle as a regular design to lay out tarot cards. This divinatory layout incorporates not only the Goddess's triangular symbol, counterclockwise circle, and three categories of past, present and future; it also has several repetitions and multiplications of her sacred number three. There was a short form of the *Yoni Yantra* utilizing only the Major Arcana, whose number 1-21 fell naturally into three division of seven cards each. The Yoni Yantra represented the door to her Holy of Holies.

The Fates were associated with the three phases of the moon and with the past, present, and future and presided over magical rites, deliveries and human births. Clothed in white gowns made from linen, the Fates marked off the days of human life with their wool; the length of the yarn determined by them. Legends tell us this magical spinning occurred at early evening to nightfall. There are three movements in making the thread and three movements or actions are involved in the process of spinning, another reason it is associated with the Fates. Their names were *Clotho*, the Spinner (the Virgin*)*, *Lacxhesis* (the Mother), and *Atropos* (the Crone).

130

NOTES

1 Regarding the origination of the name Beltane, Lawrence Durdin-Robertson speculates, "It is possible the great Celtic festival of Beltane, on May 1st, may derive its name from the first two deities of the Carthaginian Triad, *Baal*-Hammon, *Ta*nit and *E*shmun." Lawrence Durdin-Robertson, *The Year of the Goddess: A Perpetual Calender of Festivals* (Wellingborough, England: The Aquarian Press, 1990), 99.

2 Group email correspondence, Jacqueline Lasahn, April 27, 2003.

3 Hawthorn blossoms are connected to some interesting folk practices. They emit "a strong scent of female sexuality; which is why the Turks use a flowering branch as an erotic symbol." Robert Graves, *The White Goddess* (New York: The Noonday Press, 1975), 176. For associations with Jana and Diana, 68-9. "In the perpetual style of the lingam-yoni, the wreath served as the female symbol surrounding the phallic pole." Barbara Walker, *The Women's Dictionary of Symbols and Sacred Objects* (San Francisco: Harper Collins, 1988), 465. "The *thorn apple* referred either to the hawthorn or to the intensely poisonous Jimsonweed (*Datura stramonium*), which was a frequent ingredient of witches' recipes. 454. "The '*Datura stramonium* L.(*) var. *tatula Torr.*' [is a] flower offering (particularly to Shiva)." There is an illustration of a black lingam topped with a wreath and "a blossom of Datura, a flower associated with the worship of the Hindu god Shiva." Claudia Muller-Ebeling, Christian Ratsch, and Surendra Bahadur Shahi, *Shamanism and Tantra in the Himalayas* (Rochester: Inner Traditions, 2000), 152. In relation to datura and dew, there is a photograph of a bronze statue of the Buddha Amitabha seated under the jeweled tree of Paradise. Next to the illustration, it is noted, "It was believed that when Buddha preached, dew or raindrops fell from heaven on Datura." Richard Evans Schultes and Albert Hoffman, *Plants of the Gods* (New York: Alfred van der Marck Editions, 1987), 106-108.

4 Durdin-Robertson (1990), 100-101.

5 "At night, people dragged sheets across the fields collecting dew which was then used for healing." Audrius Dundzila, "Rasa: The Summer Solstice," (1991), http://www.geocities.com/Athens/Oracle/2810/rasa.html.

6 The *Kupuole* (similar to the Maypole) "was celebrated in the festival of *Raste* (or *Rasa*, 'Dew'), a two-week holiday leading up to the summer solstice. Rasa was also known as Saule's [Lithuanian Sun Goddess'] daughter. Rasa watered the vegetation with her silvery morning dew which would in turn help nourish the crops. The Lithuanians believed her morning dew had youth-giving powers, and they would wash their faces and wet their clothes with it on the solstice morning." Jeff Day, "Gods and Goddesses of the Balts," http://www. geocities.com/cas111jd/balts/balt_gods2.htm.

7 In Sanskrit, "*Tara* or *Taraka* means star (cf. Persian *Sitara*, Greek *Aster*, Latin *Stella* and English '*Star*.'" N.N. Bhattacharyya, *The Indian Mother Goddess* (Delhi, India: Manohar, 1977), 209. "Tara's name is derived from the verb *t'r*, to cross or traverse . . . the Tantras take its etymology to mean 'that which leads to the other shore.'" Alain Danielou, *The Myths and Gods of India* (Rochester: Inner Traditions, 1985), 274-277. Tara, thus, becomes the goddess who ferries across, or saves. Erich Neumann tells us she is often associated with boats (Mistress of Boats) and sometimes is even depicted as the boat itself saving her devotees from dangers, enabling them to cross the ocean of troubles. Erich Neumann, *The Great Mother* (Princeton, NJ: Princeton University Press, 1963), 333. See Appendix B for further information on Tara.

8 The moon was worshiped in ecstatic dances by priestesses. As 'mothers of the moon cult," they were believed to resemble the orgiastic maenads. Heide Gottner-Abendroth, *The Dancing Goddess* (Boston: Beacon Press, 1982), 31-34.

[9] Allan Hunt Badiner and Alex Grey, *Zig Zag Zen: Buddhism and Psychedelics* (San Francisco: Chronicle Books, 2002), 23.

[10] Andrews (1995), 132.

[11] J.E. Circlot, *A Dictionary of Symbols*, Trans. Jack Sage (New York: Dorset Press, 1971), 2d ed., 71.

[12] Andrews (1995), 130.

[13] Circlot (1971), 71.

[14] "Here at Kailash, Drolma La is Tibetan for the Tara Pass. Tara's Tear is the lake just over the pass. She's there in the pilgrim's passing by: She smiles at you from human, animal, water, rock." Robert Thurman and Tad Wise, *Circling the Sacred Mountain* (New York: Bantam Books, 1999),149. Alain Danielou describes Mt. Kalaish as "the blessed and splendid mountain where Shiva dwells . . . The mountain is of great height and its sparkling peaks sown with many coloured precious stones and other ores." It is a place (for those with the ability to see) of delight inhabited with heavenly spirits known as *kinaras*, *apsaras*, and *siddhas*, animals such as the (non-ferocious tiger, deer, and birds). It is covered with gardens, grottos and silver-hued trees and is where nature shines. Alain Danielou, *Gods of Love and Ecstasy: The Traditions of Shiva and Dionysus* (Rochester, NY: Inner Traditions, 1992), 133.

[15] "You have to ask," friend and curandera Camila Martinez reminds me speaking of the all-seeing, all-hearing, all-knowing Tara. It seems simple but we forget to ask. (Personal communication, 4-27-01).

[16] For more information on the sacred significance of the number three (and sacred geometry), Michael Schneider, *A Beginner's Guide to Constructing the Universe* (New York: Harper, 1994), 38-59.

[17] Rasa means precious dew or essence of delight.

[18] Beginner's mind is "the mind that is innocent of preconceptions and expectations, judgments and prejudices. Beginner's mind is just being present to explore and observe and see 'things as-it-is.'" Abbess Zenkei Blanche Hartman, "A Natural Action," (2000). Unpublished article, http://www.intrex.net/chzg/hartman3.htm.

[19] For a discussion on essence and personality, see the work of Ali Hammed Almaas, in particular, *Essence with The Elixir of Enlightenment: The Diamond Approach to Inner Realization* (York Beach, ME: Samuel Weiser), 1998).

[20] This pilgrimage included visits to the shrines and temples of tantric Hindu and Buddhist female deities. For an in-depth study from a pilgrimage participant's perspective, see Laura Chamberlain's Master's thesis "Embodying the Goddess Durga: A Pilgrimage to the Mother Goddess of Paradox" (California Institute of Integral Studies, 2001), Masters Abstracts International 140 (2002): 919. Accession no. AAT1407335.

[21] David Abram, *The Spell of the Sensuous* (New York: Vintage Books, 1996), 20-28.

[22] In Guru Yoga the teacher or *yidam* (yidam is the deity, i.e., Tara, dakini, *Taparitza*) is placed at the center of a disciple's practice. Taparitza is a representation of all the Bon lineage masters visualized without ornamentation and signifies the clear mind. In order to practice the teachings of the yidam, an empowerment which includes an oral transmission is required from a Lama or spiritual master.

23   In 1999, I received an empowerment to practice Simhamuka's sadhana from Tsultrim Allione. *Simhamuka* is the lion-headed wisdom dakini of the Buddhist pantheon of deities. She is fierce and compassionate. Her principal magical function is to avert negative energy. According to John Reynolds, she can be compared to the wrathful form of the Hindu goddess Durga. Instead of riding a lion, however, she is lion-faced. She represents the Crone aspect of feminine wisdom and has similarities to Sekhmet, the Egyptian lion-headed goddess who is associated with the fiery sun. Simhamuka "is the Nirmanakaya manifestation, appearing in time and history, whereas her Sambhogakaya aspect is *Vajravarahi* and her Dharmakaya aspect is *Samantabhadri*, the Primordial Wisdom herself." John Myrdhin Reynolds, "The Wrathful Lion-Headed Dakini," http://www.angelfire.com/vt/vajranatha/simha.html

24   Bon tradition is the indigenous spiritual tradition of Tibet that predates Indian Buddhism, believed to be seventeen thousand years old. For an inspiring chapter on Tara and the Bon Religion of Tibet, see Allyson Rickard, *Tara Practice: Cultivating the Chi of the Black Sect Tantric Buddhist Feng Shui Practitioner*, Unpublished manuscript (2001), 13-32.

25   Mary B. Kelly is the author of *Goddess Embroideries of Eastern Europe* (McClean, NY: StudioBooks, 1996).

26   Sheila Paine is the author of *Afghan Amulet* (New York: St. Martin's Press, 1994), and *Embroidered Textiles, Traditional Patterns from Five Continents* (London: Thames and Hudson, 1990).

27   Four hundred miles east of Moscow on the Volga River lies the land of the Chuvash. Mary B. Kelly claims a connection of the Chuvash to the legendary Amazons of the Black Sea.

28   Meditation practices during this period consisted of "mindfulness meditation," using special mantras or the breath to anchor and quiet the mind.

29   "Pilgrimage, in Jungian terms, is an expression of, and an effort to circumambulate the Self, to 'quicken the divinity' by bringing the Self within us to life," Jean Shinoda Bolen, *Crossing to Avalon* (San Francisco: Harper, 1995), 249.

30   See the work of George Quasha, *Ainu Dreams* (Barrytown, NY: Station Hill Press, 1999).

31   I borrowed this title from the book on dream work by Jeremy Taylor, *Where People Fly and Water Runs Uphill* (New York: Warner Books, 1992).

32   Buddha's mother had a dream portending his birth. As Serinity Young points out, "At the very beginning of Buddhism, dreaming is central. Indeed, without Maya's [Buddha's mother] dream there would be no Buddhas and hence no Buddhism." Serinity Young (*Dreaming the Lotus: Buddhist Dream Narrative, Imagery, and Practice* (Somerville, MA: Wisdom Publications, 1999), 24.

33   *Oxford English Dictionary* (Online) (OED). New York: University Press, 2003. http://dictionary.oed.com.

34   Robert Sigrist, "Apophatic Mysticism: The Capture of Happiness," http://www.apophaticmysticism.com/definitions.html.

35   Clark Moustakas, *Heuristic Research* (Newbury Park, CA: Sage Publications, 1990).

36 Jennifer Clements, et al.,"Organic Inquiry: If Research Were Sacred," Unpublished manuscript (1999).

37 Carl Jung's technique of amplification makes use of personal, symbolic and mythic associations for understandings of dream figures.

38 Daniel Deslauriers, "Dreamwork in the Light of Emotional and Spiritual Intelligence." *Advanced Development Journal* 9 (2000): 1–18.

39 Kelly Bulkeley, *The Wilderness of Dreams: Exploring the Religious Meanings of Dreams in Modern Western Culture* (Albany: SUNY Press, 1994), 133-180. For a discussion on root metaphors, see Chapter 3.

40 "The development of such capacities takes place over the entire life span and, as Jung (1961, 1974) and Washburn (1988) have pointed out, it takes on a special significance at, or around, middle age. During this period, one is confronted not only with personal concerns, but also a deeper level, connected to a 'collective unconsciousness.'" Deslaurier (2000), 4.

41 Marc Ian Barasch, *Healing Dreams* (New York: Penguin Putnam, 2000).

42 Stephen La Berge, *Lucid Dreaming* (New York: Ballantine Books, 1985) and Stephen La Berge and Howard Rheingold, *Exploring the World of Lucid Dreaming* (New York: Ballantine Books, 1990).

43 Mary Watkins, *Waking Dreams* (Dallas, TX: Spring Publications, Inc., 1992).

44 Kathleen Sullivan, *Recurring Dreams: A Journey to Wholeness* (Freedom: Crossing Press, 1998).

45 Kelly Bulkeley, *Spiritual Dreaming: A Cross-cultural and Historical Journey* (New York: Paulist Press, 1995), and Kelly Bulkeley, *The Wilderness of Dreams: Exploring the Religious Meanings of Dreams in Modern Western Culture* (Albany, NY: SUNY Press, 1994).

46 Rhea White, "Becoming More Human as We Work: The Reflexive Role of Exceptional Human Experience" In William Braud and Rosemarie Anderson, *Transpersonal Research Methods of the Social Sciences: Honoring Human Experience* (Thousand Oaks: Sage Publications, 1998), 128-45. Also see Rhea White's website, http://www.ehe.org/display/ehe-menu.cfm?sectid=14.

47 Yvonne Kason, M.D. and Teri Degler, *A Farther Shore: How Near-Death and Other Extraordinary Experiences Can Change Ordinary Lives* (Toronto, Canada, Harper Collins Publishers, 1994), 222-5. In these dreams, Kason reports there appears to be an increase in color perception and other sensual perceptions while dreaming. Synchronicities in dream life and waking life are also known to occur more frequently.

48 See Krippner, Bogzaran, and De Carvalho (2002), 135-45.

49 Tenzin Wangyal Rinpoche, *The Tibetan Yogas of Dream and Sleep* (Ithaca, NY: Snow Lion Publications, 1998), 62-64.

50 Jayne I. Gackenbach, former president of the Association for the Study of Dreams, reports that EEG analysis on electrical brain activity during meditative and sleep states "supports H.T. Hunt's idea that lucid dreaming [an often reported component of clarity dreams] is a form of spontaneously emerging meditation." It

appears that meditators have more lucid dreams than non-meditators and that these dreams are more transpersonal in nature and often include encounters with spiritual beings. Interestingly, Gackenbach proposes that women have a higher propensity for lucid dreams based on the female brain's neuro-electrical organization capacities. She found that regular meditation practice increases the frequency and general recall of lucid dream experiences as well as increases overall healing for these individuals, especially women. She informs us that women who have spontaneous lucid dreams often show a higher degree of inter-hemispheric specialization than those who never have lucid dreams. See Jayne I. Gackenbach "Women and Meditators as Gifted Lucid Dreamers," in Krippner, Stanley, ed. *Dreamtime & Dreamwork*, New York: Tarcher Putnam, 1990, 244-251. Also H. T. Hunt, *The Multiplicity of Dreams: A Cognitive Psychological Perspective* (New Haven, CT: Yale University Press, 1989).

[51] Namkhai Norbu, *Dream Yoga and the Practice of Natural Light* (Ithaca, NY: Snow Lion, 1992), 26.

[52] Ibid., "Startling, creative or transcendent outcomes often emerge from these special dreams, some of which may be channeled."

[53] Stephen La Berge, *Lucid Dreaming: The Power of Being Awake & Aware in Your Dreams* (New York: Ballantine Books, 1985).

[54] Yvonne Kason, M.D. and Teri Degler, *A Farther Shore: How Near-Death and Other Extraordinary Experiences Can Change Ordinary Lives* (Toronto, Canada: Harper Collins Publishers, 1994), 28.

[55] David Abram, *The Spell of the Sensuous* (New York: Vintage Books, 1996), 59-62.

[56] Diana L. Eck, *Darsan* (Chambersburg, PA: Anima Books, 1985).

[57] Krippner, Bogzaran, and de Carvalho (2002), 157-158.

[58] Ibid., 135-45.

[59] Ibid., 137.

[60] Jana was a name once used by women to designate their guardian angel. Barbara Walker, *The Women's Dictionary of Symbols and Sacred Objects* (San Francisco: Harper Collins, 1988), 208-209; Barbara Walker, *The Women's Encyclopedia of Myths and Secrets* (Edison, NJ: Castle Books, 1996), 339, 461.

[61] Rudolph Otto, *The Idea of the Holy* (Trans. John W. Harvey, Oxford, England: Oxford University Press, 2d ed., 1950).

[62] Tom Gunning, "Sacredness," http://www.materdei.ie/logos/sacredness%20article.htm.

[63] Ibid.

[64] Matthew Fox and Rupert Sheldrake, *The Physics of Angels: Exploring the Realm Where Science and Spirit Meet* (San Francisco: Harper San Francisco, 1996).
[65] Ibid., vii.

[66] Ibid., 178-179. Rupert Sheldrake quoting Hildegard of Bingen, J. P. Migne, ed. Patrologia Latina (Paris: Migne, 1844-91), 197, 1043C.

[67] Ibid., 178-179.

[68] "Astonishingly, not many studies have been written on shape-shifting" states Catharina Raudvere, "Now You See Her, Now You Don't: Some Notes on the Conception of Female Shape-Shifters in Scandinavian Traditions" in Sandra Billington and Miranda Green, eds, *The Concept of the Goddess* (London: Routledge, 1996), 48.

[69] In a lecture from a course, "Beginning Sanskrit," (Fall Semester, 2001), California Institute of Integral Studies, San Francisco, Professor Jim Ryan spoke about how Sanskrit Vedic hymns were chanted forwards, backwards and from the middle out by Hindu priests.

[70] David Coxhead and Susan Hiller, *Dreams: Visions of the Night* (New York: Crossroad Publishing Company 1976) for examples of *ittals*. A counter-clockwise spiral dance is illustrated in an *ittal* owned by author.

[71] Abram (1996), 5. Also see Elizabeth Barber, *Prehistoric Textiles* (Princeton: Princeton University Press, 1991), 37 discusses the spirit world and reversals.

[72] James Hillman, *The Soul's Code* (New York: Random House, 1996), 139.

[73] Walker (1996), 339.

[74] In a lecture from course, "Ecology, Consciousness, and Society" (3-16-01) by Professor Ralph Metzner, California Institute of Integral Studies, San Francisco.

[75] Ralph Metzner, *TheUnfolding Self: Varieties of Transformative Experience* (Novato, CA: Origin Press, 1998), 132-133.

[76] "Although there have been many books written on the general topic of dreams, there has still been relatively little that would serve to bring dream work into the spiritual context. Buddhist, Bonpo and Taoist teachers have acknowledged to me that this situation has influenced their decisions to teach more openly." Michael Katz, Introduction to *Dream Yoga and the Practice of Natural Light*, Namkhai Norbu (Ithaca: Snow Lion, 1992), 29.

[77] Sven Doehner, "Sound Transformation in Dream-Work: Nourishing the Soul," Unpublished article, 2002.

[78] Daniel Goleman, *Emotional Intelligence* (New York: Bantam Books, 1995).

[79] The Women's Spirituality Movement and the field of Ecopsychology address these concerns.

[80] Daniel Deslaurier, "Dreamwork in the Light of Emotional and Spiritual Intelligence" published in *Advanced Development Journal*, 2000, 4.

[81] Deslaurier quoting Roger Lipsey, *An Art of Our Own: The Spiritual in Twentieth Century Art* (Boston: Shambala, 1988) in Deslaurier, "Dreamwork in the Light of Emotional and Spiritual Intelligence" published in *Advanced Development Journal*, 2000, 4.

[82] Ibid., 2.

83   C. Kerenyi. *Asklepios* (New York: Bollingen Foundation, 1959). Also see Carl Alfred Meier, *Healing Dream and Ritual* (Einsiedeln: Daimon Verlag, 1989). In the healing centers, dreams were incubated. The treatments included bathing for purification, fasting and sleeping in the temple. A vision of a god, goddess, or numen was sought. A message from the dream visitation was interpreted by a priest and used in the preparation of prescriptions for healings.

84   Stephen Aizenstat, "DreamTending: Befriending the Archetypal Imagination," abstract, Association for the Study of Dreams (ASD) Conference Program, Sept. 21- Oct. 5, 2003, Oakland, California, 2003.

85   Krippner, et al, 165, referring to Charles Tart's article "World simulation in waking and dreaming," in *Journal of Mental Imagery* 11 (1987), 145-158.

86   Krippner, et al, 165.

87   See the ASD, Association for the Study of Dreams, http://www.asdreams.org/.

88   See Michael Katz's introduction to *Dream Yoga* by Namkahi Norbu, 33.

89   *Oxford English Dictionary* (Online) (OED). New York: University   Press, 2002. http://dictionary.oed.com.

90   J. A. Hobson, *The Dreaming Brain*, (New York: Basic Books, 1988).

91   See Kelly Bulkeley and Wendy Doniger, "Why Study Dreams? A Religious Studies Perspective," *Dreaming.* 3: no.1, (1993): 69; Deslauriers (2000).

92   Katz, Introduction to *Dream Yoga* by Namkai Norbu (1992), 23-24.

93   Serinity Young states in one dream a dakini transmitted to Namkai Norbu tantras. ". . . he dreamed that the goddess Tara told him where to find a female ascetic who 'could tell him all that he wished to know.'" Serinity Young, *Dreaming in the Lotus* (Boston: Wisdom Publications, 1999), 107.

94   Ibid.

95   Deslauriers (2000), 4.

96   Ibid, 8.

97   'Spiritually Transformative Experience' is a term coined by Yvonne Kason. Yvonne Kason, M.D. and Teri Degler. *A Farther Shore: How Near-Death and Other Extraordinary Experiences Can Change Ordinary Lives* (Toronto, Canada: Harper Collins Publishers, 1994), 17-26.

98   'Exceptional Human Experience' is a term coined by Rhea White. See Rhea White, "Becoming More Human as We Work: The Reflexive Role of Exceptional Human Experience,' In *Transpersonal Research Methods of the Social Sciences: Honoring Human Experience* by William Braud and Rosemarie Anderson (Thousand Oaks, CA: Sage Publications, 1998), 128-45; and http://www.ehe.org/display/ehe-menu.cfm?sectid=14.

99   Ali Hammed Almaas, *Essence with The Elixir of Enlightenment: The Diamond Approach to Inner Realization* (York Beach, ME: Samuel Weiser, Inc., 1998).

100   Jean Houston, *A Mythic Life: Learning to Live Our Greater Story* (New York, Harper Collins Publishers, 1996), 124-127.

101   Marsha Sinetar quoted in Beatrix Murrell, "Noetic Gnosis: Cosmic Consciousness," http://www.csp.org/experience/docs/noetic_gnosis.html.

102   Stanislav Grof, *The Holotropic Mind* (New York: HarperCollins, 1992), 160.

103   James Hillman, *The Soul's Code: In Search of Character and Calling* (New York: Random House, 1996), 8.

104   Ibid.

105   Serinity Young, *Dreaming in the Lotus* (Boston: Wisdom Publications, 1999), 107.

106   Ibid., 143.

107   Ibid.

108   Ibid.

109   I was fortunate to have studied this method directly with one of its founders, Dianne Jenett, Ph.D.

110   Clements (2002), 14.

111   Alan Watts, *The Way of Zen* (Toronto: Vintage Books, 1957).

112   Lucia Birnbaum, *Black Madonnas: Feminism, Religion, & Politics in Italy* (Boston: Northeastern University Press, 1993) and Lucia Birnbaum, *Dark Mother: African Origins and Godmothers* (Lincoln, NE: iUniverse, 2001).

113   Birnbaum (1993), (2001).

114   Birnbaum (1993), (2001), (2003), and Anica Vesel Mander, *Blood Ties* (New York: Random House, 1976).

115   Clements, et al. (1999), 51.

116   See Abraham Maslow, *Religion, Values, and Peak Experiences* (New York: Viking), 1964; Michael Polanyi, *The Tacit Dimension* (Garden City: Doubleday, 1966); Eugene Gendlin, Focusing (New York: Everest House, 1978); Martin Buber, *The Knowledge of Man* (New York: Harper & Row, 1950); P.N. Bridgman, *Reflections of a Physicist* (New York: Philosophical Library, 1950); Carl Rogers, *Client-centered Therapy* (Boston: Houghton-Mifflin), 1951.

117 Braud & Anderson state, "Many of the most significant and exciting life events and extraordinary experiences—moments of clarity, illumination, and healing—have been systematically excluded from conventional research." William Braud and Rosemarie Anderson, *Transpersonal Research Methods of the Social Sciences: Honoring Human Experience.*Thousand Oaks, CA: Sage Publications, 1998, 3.

118 Clark Moustakas, *Heuristic Research* (Newbury Park, CA: Sage, 1990).

119 Ibid., 11.

120 Other qualitative methods "insists that the researcher identify and bracket her or his assumptions and presuppositions to achieve a state of that is free of personal judgment." Jennifer Clements, Dorothy Ettling, Dianne Jenett, and Lisa Shields, "If Research Were Sacred–An Organic Methodology," http://www.serpentina.com/research-x.html.

121 Discoveries in brain research indicate the left hemisphere is largely concerned with the rational, logical, critical, and censorial mind—the clear-cut definable units, definitions, classifications into definable units. By contrast the right hemisphere, "constantly thinks in complex images; it patterns to make designs of whatever it encounters . . . it lends itself to the formation of original ideas, insights, discoveries . . . it is the kind of thought prevalent in early childhood, when everything is new and everything has meaning." Gabriele Lusser Rico, *Writing the Natural Way: Using Right-Brain Techniques to Release Your Expressive Powers* (Los Angeles: J.P. Tarcher, 1983), 17-18.

122 Eugene T. Gendlin, *Focusing* (New York: Everest House, 1978).

123 Clark Moustakas, *Heuristic Research* (Newbury Park, CA: Sage, 1990), 25.

124 Rico (1983), 35-43.

125 Clark Moustakis states, "The question or statement must be exact as it will determine whether or not an authentic and compelling path has opened, one that will sustain the researcher's curiosity, involvement, and participation with full energy and resourcefulness over a lengthy period of time." Moustakis (1990), 40.

126 Braud and Anderson (1998), xxvii.

127 Judith M. Meloy, *Writing the Qualitative Dissertation: Understanding by Doing* (Mahwah, NJ: Lawrence Erlbaum Assoc., Publishers, 2002), xiii.

128 Beverly Moon, ed., *An Encyclopedia of Archetypal Symbolism* (Boston: Shambhala, 1991), xvi.

129 Moustakis (1990), 12.

130 Kelly Bulkeley, *The Wilderness of Dreams: Exploring the Religious Meanings of Dreams in Modern Western Culture* (Albany, NY: SUNY Press, 1994), 113.

131 Braud and Anderson (1998), 80.

132 Ibid.

133 Nada Yoga works with the emotions through toning. Toning acts as a bridge between form and the formless. It's goal is to purify and magnetize, activate and balance the chakras. When done correctly, one is able to release and heal repressed emotions and become receptive to subtle vibrations. When working with emotions through the voice, each note is meant to correspond to a particular emotion. By using this technique, one is also able to find one's own natural voice, or note that resonates for them.

134 Louise Dianne Baumgartner, *Erotic Wisdom*. Master's thesis, California Institute of Integral Studies, 1998. Masters Abstracts International 37 (1999): 1726.

135 Authentic Movement developed by Mary Whitehouse in 1965 is a method born from dance, Jungian studies and movement therapy.

136 Clements, et al. (1999), 52-3.

137 Personal conversation with Professor Cindy Shearer, April 4, 2003.

138 Tathang Tulku, *Openness Mind* (Berkeley: Dharma Press, 1978), 77 quoted in *Exploring the World of Lucid Dreaming* by Stephen LaBerge and Howard Rheingold (New York: Ballantine Books, 1990), 232.

139 Ibid., 90.

140 Ibid., 76.

141 Yogi Hari, "Yoga–The Yoga of Sound," http://www.yogihari.com/nada-yoga.htm.

142 Steven Halpern, "Spectrum Suite," Produced by Halpern Sounds, Belmont, CA, 1979.

143 Sven Doehner, Unpublished manuscript, 2003, Mexico City.

144 Anodea Judith, *Wheels of Life: A User's Guide to the Chakra System* (St. Paul, MN: Llewellyn Publications, 1987), 264.

145 Robert Temple, *The Genius of China: 3,000 Years of Science, Discovery and Invention* (New York: Simon & Schuster, 1986), 207.

146 See Appendix A: Selected Dreams.

147 Silvia Nakkach, "Sacred Sound, the Creator and the Transformer," http://www.voxmundiproject.com/sacredsound.html.

148 "It seems that, in prehistoric India, Shiva (the Benevolent) was called "Ann," a name also attributed to the goddess, the meaning of which is not known, but may be compared with the Hittite Ann, Canaanite Anat, and Celtic Anas (who became Saint Anne in Brittany)." Danielou (1992), 49-50.

149 Alain Danielou claims the Dravidians were the first group to worship Shiva. Considering the towns of the Harrapan Civilization were founded around 3800 B.C. to 1800 B.C., it is believed that Shivaism was the principal religion of the Indus Valley. Centers of the pre-Aryan Dravidian culture were prominent in what is

present day Pakistan. The Dravidians also lived on Crete. It is important to note the trade between the Indus Valley and Crete, Troy, Ur and Lagash around 2370 to 2100 B.C., Danielou (1992), 20-24.

[150] Ibid., (1992), 12.

[151] Danielou (1985), 348.

[152] Ibid., 334.

[153] Ibid.

[154] Group email from Layne Redmond, 1-3-03.

[155] Vac was acknowledged as a purifying presence. In the Rg-Veda she is also described as "the inciter of all pleasant songs, all gracious thought, and every pious thought." She is the goddess who inspired the *rsis* and reveals herself through speech. Vac is in fact considered to be speech itself; "The mysteries and miracles of speech express her peculiar numinous nature." She is also the prompter and vehicle for the perception of visions. David R. Kinsley, *The Hindu Goddesses* (Berkeley: University of California Press, 1988) 10-12.

[156] Ibid. Saraswati is often identified with Vac and Vagdevi in the Brahmanas. In later Hinduism, Saraswati is increasingly associated with speech, creative sound, culture (the arts) and learning.

[157] June Campbell, *Traveller in Space* (New York: George Braziller, Inc., 1996), 132.

[158] Ibid.

[159] Janet Gyatso, "Down with the Demoness: Reflections on a Feminine Ground in Tibet" in Janice Willis, ed., *Feminine Ground* (Ithaca: Snow Lion Publications, 1987), 253.

[160] The CD, *The Sacred Chants of Shiva from the Banks of the Ganges*, (Singers of the Art of Living, Produced by Craig Pruess, www.sonarupa.co.uk/itm00674.htm, includes: 1) the chant "Shiva Manas Puja," a prayer for cutting attachments, an offering to Shiva, the embodiment of pure consciousness, knowledge, innocence and bliss; 2) "Bhavanyastakam," *astakams* or prayers to Mother Divine; 3) "Shivoham," a chant expressing the enlightened wisdom that Shiva is one's innermost self . . . innocent, blissful, splendid, golden, beautiful. My innermost nature and form is Shiva. I am always there. Even though the body dies, I am always there. I am eternal. My breath is everywhere. I am formless though I am inside a form, move in forms. I am lively, full of life, consciousness; 4) "Atmastakam," a song that expresses the individual soul is one with Shiva; 5) "Lingashtakam," a chant to honor the formless aspects of Shiva and; 6) "Om Nama Shivaya," the universal sound of Shiva.

[161] Coleman Barks, from poem "Where Everything is Music" in *The Essential Rumi* (San Francisco: Harper, 1995), 34.

[162] My translator in Moscow, Nina Tortunova, explained to me the city was built in concentric circles, like circles of mothers.

[163] Hubbs (1988), xii.

164 "There once and forever lived a woman who spun words of wisdom from gossamer thread so fine that the eye could not see, so soft that only the breeze could hear, so strong that it cut through eons of hard silence." Dr. Lucia Birnbaum quoting from a leaflet distributed by Steelekha, a feminist bookstore in Bangalore, India. Lucia Birnbaum, *Dark Mother: African Origins and Godmothers* (Lincoln, NE: iUniverse, 2001) 356.

165 "Being in your ancestral place helps you know . . . Our grandmother's everyday spiritual ways of knowing are central in knowing who we are, as well as crucial to our understanding of history. . . . Each of us comes into the world with eyes we inherit from our grandparents and parents; i.e., knowledge given to us genetically, maybe in the DNA inherited from our mothers . . . . Vision may be enhanced by studying our ethnic, family, and cultural histories, particularly studying our ancestral places on-site . . . . Vision may be widened by knowledge offered to us by others (scholars, colleagues, teachers, students, birds, animals, et al)." Birnbaum (2003), 12-16.

166 Some Slavic peoples retain some linguistic connection to ancient non-Slavic peoples with one fascinating connection between the Bulgars of antiquity and the Volga Bulgars, Crimean Tatars, and Tatars of today in some roots and personal names. Wickpedia. "Slavic Peoples," http://www.wikipedia.org/wiki/Slavic people.

167 Russian women—Batyukova Natalia Ivanovna, Kozlova Zinaida, Gudkova Tatyana Ivanovna and Zakharova Vera Nikovaevna—informed me chevrons represented fire; meanders designated water; swastikas, the sun; triangles, the cross, and diamond, "woman beginning;" labyrs, instrument to plow; the double furka referred to the garden; the "M" with a vertical line going through it was "'wings of the bird;" an upside down "U" was the sky, and hooks meant "land to plow."

168 Many of the patterns are reminiscent of early Neolithic pottery designs, many which are illustrated in the work of Marija Gimbutas, *The Civilization of the Goddess: The World of Old Europe* (San Francisco, Harper, 1991); *The Goddesses and Gods of Old Europe, Myths and Cult Images* (Berkeley, CA: University of California Press, 1982); *The Language of the Goddess* (San Francisco: Harper Collins, 1991); *The Living Goddesses*. Edited by Miriam Robbins Dexter (Berkeley: University of California Press, 1999).

169 Philippa Rappoport, "Doll Folktales of the East Slavs: Invocation of Women from the Boundary of Space and Time." Ph.D. diss., University of Virginia, 1997, Dissertation Abstracts International 59 (1998): 509. Accession no. AAT9824292, 70.

170 "The bathhouse and the rozhanitsy were the center of the cult of the family, and in Kievan and Muscovite Russia, old women were censured by the priesthood most particularly for the special feasts which they prepared in honor of the goddesses of fate who presided over childbirth." Hubbs (1988), 15.

171 *Piatnitsa* whose name means Friday is associated with the orgiastic pagan cult. The day of worship was Friday. Malgorzata Oleszkiewicz, "Mother of God and Mother Earth: Religion, Gender and Transformation in East-Central Europe" Unpublished manuscript, The University of Texas, 10-11.

172 Danielou (1992).

173 Richard Stoney offers an in-depth study on Zhiva / Shiva including a possible connection of Zhiva to the goddess *Bhavani*. Richard Stoney, "Shiva-Shakti Pattern," http://geocities.com/richston2/ssp, htm. Another interesting note I discovered is the name "Chuvash" is believed by some to have derived from "civas," "sivas," "savas."

174 Marija Gimbutas, *The Balts* (London: Thames and Hudson Ltd., 1963).

175 Janet Farrar and Stewart Farrar, "The Witches' Goddess,
http://web.raex.com/~gbuckley/BOS/GG/Goddess.htm.

176 Baba Yaga / Jedza / Czarownica or *wiedzma* (which comes from the Polish *wiedziec* meaning to know, *wiedza* knowledge. She embodies the chthonic, fertility and all-encompassing goddess unlike the the Virgin Mary in the West whose uncontrollable aspects of wisdom, sexuality, dominion over death, and magical transformational powers have been eradicated and incorporates only the virgin and motherhood aspects. Mary's officially emphasized qualities are submission, humility, purity, suffering, and renunciation. For centuries these qualities have been used as a model for women in the western world, depriving them of their power. (When I was in Moscow, my interpreter and guide Nina Tortunova informed me no one ever refers to the Mother as the Virgin Mary, only Mary, Mother of God). Regarding the old woman, even old age in its capacity to free women from the control of men, has been demonized. Old women are either witches, Yagas, or *baby*, a derogative name for a married or old woman in Poland and Russia; originally pertinent to the goddess Zlota Baba. Even though Baba Yaga has been demonized, she still retains her positive qualities in folktale in which she is both good and bad, young and old. Malgorzata Oleszkiewicz, "Mother of God and Mother Earth: Religion, Gender and Transformation in East-Central Europe,"Unpublished manuscript (The University of Texas, n.d.), 4-8. For a rendering of the Vasalisa / Baba Yaga folktale as a girl's initiation story, see Clarissa Pinkola Estes, *Women Who Run with the Wolves: Myths and Stories of the Wild Woman Archetype* (New York: Ballantine Books, 1992), 74–114.

177 Rappoport (1998), ii–iii, v.; Also wooden dolls used by the Lapps, idols containing spirits are called *seidi*, "recalling the Sanskrit *siddhi*, magical spirit. Walker (1988), 93.

178 Rappoport (1998), 7-8. Along with dolls as magic objects, spittle, spindles and 'talking buns,' considered under the rubric of unclean forces, were used as apotropaic devices.

179 Ibid., 3.

180 Wayne Schlepp, "Cinderella in Tibet," *Asian Folklore Studies Nagoya*: 61: no. 1, (2002), 123.

181 Ibid. A repository of stories brought together within a main story which a prince and disciple of Narajuna is on a journey to find a corpse that will promise salvation of the world. Through the course of secret rituals and observances, he finds the corpse and proceeds to remove it from the cemetery. The corpse tells stories to the Prince while being abducted (stories with surprise endings) so that the corpse is able to fly away.

182 Ibid., 61.

183 Ibid., 62.

184 Ibid.

185 Juno, Queen of Heaven, once the two *Janae*, was also associated with thunder. (Ibid., 63).

186 Twenty-one was long regarded as a magical number because its only multiplicands were the sacred numbers three and seven, associated with the Triple Goddess and her Pleiadic priestesses, the Seven Sisters, known in Syria and the Seven Pillars of Wisdom. By ancient tradition, each human life was normally divided into three trimesters of twenty-one years apiece foreshadowed by the three prenatal trimesters. Tarot cards clearly associated the first third of life with the past leg of the triangle, the second third with the present leg, and the last third with the future leg.

187 "Intuition is the treasure of a woman's psyche. It is like a divining instrument and like a crystal through which one can see with uncanny interior vision. It is like a wise woman who is with you always, who tells you exactly what the matter is, tells you exactly whether you need to go left or right." Pinkola Estes (1992), 74.

188 Ibid., 75.

189 A *tumi* is a golden Pre-Columbian ritual knife.

190 On *samadhi* as ecstasy, Georg Feuerstein *The Yoga Tradition* (Prescott: Hohm Press, 2001), 252-254

191 Walker (1988), 32.

192 Ibid., 245-246.

193 Fairies shrank in size over the years until they became smaller than humans.

194 I am reminded of the goddess *Hariti* in Nepal, protector of children.

195 Matthew Fox and Rupert Sheldrake. *The Physics of Angels: Exploring the Realm Where Science and Spirit Meet* (San Francisco: Harper, 1996), 5.

196 Ibid.

197 Walker (1988).

198 Ibid.

199 Ibid., 250.

200 Walker (1988), 405.

201 Ibid., 516.

202 Ibid., 209. One juno known for her sexual appetite, Juno Caprotina, "was invoked in fertility rites to fructify the fig trees."

203 Ibid., 250.

204 Prane Dunduliene, "Ancient Lithuanian Mythology and Religion," http://www.litnet.lt/litinfo/religion.html.

205 Mircea Eliade (1960), 100.

206 Marija Gimbutas, *The Language of the Goddess* (Harper: San Francisco, 1991), 239.

207 Shoymanas are believed to have abilities to possess women. Symptoms of falling under a shoymana's trance include a physical feeling of sickness. A women who feels that she may fall into trance, makes the bed, performs a ritual bath, and dresses herself in clean white clothing. Before the trance the woman sings a melancholic song. The most frequent one is a moon song dedicated to the Goddess Yana—local version of the Goddess Diana. Trance begins with pain in legs, arms, chest, stomach, and with the breaking and lowering of the temperature. During the trance, women travel through the space and time and talk with supernatural beings. Women who fall into trance are great sorceresses, but their knowledge and skills are learned during trance and not from other sorceresses. Besides rituals, they learn about healing and herbs. Among their ritual equipment are various grains, dissolved lead, mirrors. Shoymanas possess pebble stones, powerful amulets decorated with strange ornaments believed to be prints of the Goddess and "sainte" rings used for protection from other dimensional energies, for prophecy and exorcism, and from non-human intelligences which exist in other worlds or dimensions. Herbs associated with them are Roman chamomile (Anthemis nobilis), wormwood (Artemisia absinthium), geranium (Geranium macrorrhisum), and Dwarf Elder (Sambucus ebulas). Frater Gwydion,"Shoymanas: The Queens of Air," http://www.geocities.com/Athens/Agora/8933/shoymanas.html.

208 Malgorzata Oleszkiewicz, "Mother of God and Mother Earth: Religion, Gender and Transformation in East-Central Europe" (Unpublished manuscript, The University of Texas), n.d., 10.

209 Vily were female spirits who lived in the forest, mountains, and clouds known for their shapeshifting abilities. They were known to change into swans, horses, falcons, or wolves. The Siren is depicted in iconography as a woman with body, feet, and tail of a bird; breasts, face, and arms of a woman; sometimes holding a branch in one hand, or wearing a vest. She is a good luck sign, friendly, not a mermaid, but a crowned kind bird woman who inhabits the waters of mountain streams and attracts people to the water. Elizabeth Wayland Barber, "On the Origins of the *vily/ rusalki*." *In Varia on the Indo-European Past: Papers in Memory of Marija Gimbutas*, edited by Miriam Robbins Dexter and Edgar C. Polome, 6-47. Washington, DC: Institute of the Study of Man, 1997; and for the birdwoman's connection to the extra-long sleeve, Elizabeth Wayland Barber, "The Curious Tale of the Ultra-Long Sleeve," *In Folk Dress in Europe and Anatolia*, edited by Linda Welters, 111-134. New York: Berg, 1999.

210 Mary B. Kelly, *Goddess Embroideries of Eastern Europe* (McClean: StudioBooks, 1996), 11.

211 "Women brought their *prialki* (spinning distaffs) down to the river each year so she could spin clothes for herself. Prialki were in fact considered the goddess in the form of a distaff, women painted her image on them. She also lived in the cleft of a tree made by lightening. In ancient harvest rituals, a flower-wreathed girl with arms in 'orant' or upraised position is serenaded while led around the village. She is clothed in red scarves and makes movements with hands while holding wooden spoons. Berehinia Motifs: life signs, water signs, birds and birch trees. Shown with three flowers or holding two with one over her head, she eventually becomes a mermaid, sometimes shown as single or double-tailed in woodcarvings, window sils, lintels. Bird motif often appear in Polish paper cuttings with goddess depicted with bird on head." Mary B. Kelly, *Goddess Embroideries of Eastern Europe* (McClean: StudioBooks, 1996), 14.

212 Hubbs relates Procopious' account of the ancient veneration of nymphs by the Western Slavs, a religion without priests that revolved around the goddess Zhiva. Deep in the forest at the shores of rivers or lakes, ceremonies were held by the whole community. "It is thought that, as in later Russian peasant rituals, the women, both young and old, officiated." Joanna Hubbs, *Mother Russia, The Feminine Myth in Russian Culture* (Bloomington, Indiana: Indiana University Press, 1988), 13.

213 Prane Dunduliene, "Ancient Lithuanian Mythology and Religion, http://www.litnet.lt/litinfo/religion.html.

214 Sanskrit dictionaries define the word *dakini* to mean female ogre but the corresponding term in Tibetan "khandro" means "sky journeying lady." June Campbell, *Traveler in Space* (New York: George Braziller, Inc. 1996), 38.

215 Gyatso, Janet, *Apparitions of the Self* (Princeton: Princeton University Press 1998), 243.

216 Miranda Shaw, *Passionate Enlightenment* (Princeton: Princeton University Press 1994), 38-9.

217 Gyatso (1998), xxviii.

218 According to Russian scholar Kuznetzov, "Bon was introduced to Tibet in the fifth century BC when there occurred a mass migration of Iranians, from Sogdiani in north-east Iran, to the northern parts of Tibet. The theory is that they brought with them their religion, an ancient form of polytheistic Mithraism and the Aramaic alphabet (named after Aramaiti, the Iranian Earth Goddess)." June Campbell, *Traveller in Space* (New York: George Braziller, Inc., 1996), 37. It is believed that Bon originated in the west in the areas of Zhang-Zhung, bordering on what is now Pakistan.The Inner Bon, named "The New Translation School of Zhang Zhung" was found to be in harmony with the teachings of Buddhism. Later, a corrupt form of Bon called Gyu Bon grew in strength. Gyalwa Changchub and Namkhai Nyingpo, *Lady of the Lotus-Born: The Life and Times of Yeshe Tsogyal*, Translated by Padmakara Translation Group (Boston: Shambala, 1999), 104-25.

219 Campbell discusses the early worship of Mitra, the Sky Goddess from fourteenth century BC northern Mesopotania (the goddess Mitra was connected to the Anatolian goddess Ma) who eventually became subsumed by gender transformation into Mithra, the sun god. As Mithraism developed it became a male cult and anti-female. Thus, it is believed when Mithraism entered Tibet around fifth century B.C., it had likely entered with masculinist tendencies which would have had an impact on the existing shamanic traditions. Campbell (1996), 35-51.

220 Walker (1988), 239.

221 The notion that Buddhist Tantricism reversed these roles indicates a possible sublimation of female power of the matrifocal or matrilineal cultural structures of the existing indigenous tribes. Eventually, the tulku system which elevated the status of the male contributed to the weakening of the earlier archaic position of "manifestations of female identity, as they were reflected in the ancient Tantric texts of India." Campbell, (1996), 48. Vicki Noble discusses Amazons, tantric female sexuality and dakinis in *Double Goddess* (Rochester, NY: Bear & Co., 2003)

222 June Campbell (1996), 38-9. It is interesting to note that much earlier, an image of Anahita depicted on a Sumerian seal shows her on top of her consort, "identical with Kali's love-and-death sacramental posture." Anahita, "Queen of the Stars," a form of Astarte, was a form of the great goddess worshipped by the Iranians.

223 Tsultrim Allione, *Women of Wisdom* (London: Arkana, 1984), 42.

224 Ibid., 43.

225 Changchub (1999), xxxvi.

226 Allione (1984), 43.

227 Keith Dowman, *Sky Dancer* (London: Arkana, 1984), x.

[228] Young (1999), 151.

[229] Gyatso (1998), 258.

[230] Allione (1984), 132.

[231] June Campbell, 130. *Ngayah Khandro Ling*, or dakini Pure Land is the destination of Yeshe Tsoygel, as well as Padmasambhava, Milarepa, Machig Labdrom. It is in this land one gives and receives initiations.

[232] Miranda Shaw, *Passionate Enlightenment* (Princeton: Princeton University Press, 1994), 41.

[233] Matrikas mean mothers as in *asta matrikas* (eight mothers). In Hinduism, however, there is another meaning to this word. Matrika represents the power of sound, the power of the sound of the letters of the Sanskrit alphabet. Matrikas are known to arise from the heart and inner speech. When it is said there is nothing but matrika, it means the matrika creates the outer and the inner worlds. It also means sound. See *Nothing Exists That Is Not Shiva* by Swami Muktananda, (South Fallsburg: Siddha Yoga Publications, 1997).

[234] Organic Inquiry supports the open-ended outcome of an investigation.

[235] Eugene Gendlin, *Focusing* (New York: Everest House, 1978).

[236] Clark Moustakas, *Heuristic Research* (Newbury Park: Sage, 1990), 13.

[237] Julia Cameron, *The Vein of Gold: The Journey to Your Creative Heart* (New York: Jeremy P. Tharcher, 1996), 25. "Walking opens us up. It feeds us. Image by image . . . If I am snagged on a story line, I walk it out." Ibid., 26. "Walking is an exercise in heightened listening; as we walk, we awaken our neural pathways and make them more sensitive." Ibid., 28. "Listen to the land . . . it can speak to us and guide us if we are able to open ourselves to it. Walking allows us to explore such multisensory guidance from the physical world." Ibid, 29. "[Listen] to the ancestral voices that speak through landscapes. . . The 'trail' of music is both what we hear and what we make as we walk. Like the ancestors before us, we name our experience as we walk. We name both our internal and our external landscape. We have an experience of resonance, of 'sounding out' our lives in relation to the physical world." Ibid, 30.

[238] I use this term allegorically. The kingdom of Uddiyana, from the Sanskrit root *uddiyana* means "royal garden."' It was the ancient Shangri-la in northeastern India (presently northern Pakistan circa 7th century A.D.) of 'tantra par excellence,' often referred to as a magical place, a paradise on earth. A sisterhood of priestesses dedicated to spiritual development and harmonious living lived there. Practices of sound transformation using mantras and other methods existed in Uddiyana. See http://www.dharmafellowship.org/uddiyana.htm.

[239] Tricia Grame, "Life into Art; Art into Life: Transformative Effects of the Female Symbol on a Contemporary Woman Artist." Ph.D. diss., California Institute of Integral Studies, 2000. Dissertation Abstracts International 61 (2000): 3806.

[240] Sharon Williams, "A Path into the Forest." Ph.D. diss., California Institute of Integral Studies, 2002. Dissertation Abstracts International 63 (2002): 622. Accession no. AAT3042881

241 Mari Pat Ziolkowski, "Fierce Shakti/Fierce Love: A Feminist, Heuristic, Transpersonal Encounter with the Hindu Goddess Kali Ma." Ph.D. diss., California Institute of Integral Studies, 2003. Dissertation Abstracts International 64 (2003): 309. Accession no. AAT3078806

242 Susan Gail Carter, "Amaterasu-O-Mi-Kami, Past and Present: An Exploration of the Japanese Sun Goddess from a Western Feminist Perspective." Ph.D. diss., California Institute of Integral Studies, 2001. Dissertation Abstracts International 62/02 (2001): 803. Accession no. AAT3004465

243 "Submerged knowledge, I have discovered, may hide in folklore." Birnbaum, "Dark wheat and red poppies," Unpublished paper, 6-21-03, 8.

244 Stanislav Grof and Christina Grof, *Spiritual Emergency: When Personal Transformation Becomes a Crisis* (Los Angeles, Jeremy P. Tharcher, Inc., 1989).

245 See Appendix B for information on pilgrimages.

246 Steven Halpern and Louis Savary, *Sound Health* (San Francisco: Harper & Row, 1985), 164. See Steven Halpern's website, http://innerpeacemusic.com for more information on sound and selections of CD's. Accessed on 11/2/03.

247 Carl Jung used the term "big dreams" to refer to extraordinary dreams that contained archetypal content.

248 I chose the numbers three and nine for their sacred significance. Three is the triple goddess, also known for beginning, middle, end, and many more associations. See Michael Schneider, *A Beginner's Guide to Constructing the Universe* (New York: Harper, 1994), 39-59. "There are nine celestial spheres, and nine degrees in the hierarchy of the angels. Moreover, nine corresponds, geometrically, to the circumference of the circle and therefore to the movements of the heavenly bodies and to the visible form of the firmament which is itself the great symbol of Heaven." Martin Ling, *Symbol & Archetype: A Study of Meaning of Existence* (Cambridege, U.K..:Quinta essentia, 1991), 92-3. Also, there are nine muses and nine rasas.

249 There is a Balinese legend about Shiva and flutes. "Lord Shiva once sat on Mount Meru . . . Out of the distance, he heard soft tones of a kind he had never heard before. He summoned Narada, the wise man, sending him to the Himalayan hermitage to find out where the tones were coming from. Narada went on his way and finally researched the hermitage of the sage Dereda. The hermit told him that the wondrous tones, indeed, were coming from his land. The hermitage was surrounded by a bamboo grove. Dereda had made holes in the bamboo canes to tie them together. Now, when the wind blew through the holes, the most diverse tones would be sounded. Dereda said he had been so delighted by this discovery that he had tied a bunch of bamboo canes with holes together and hung them up in a tree (creating a sound box like an aeolian harp), for no other reason than to produce a continual, pleasant sound. Narada returned to Lord Shiva to report to him what he had learned. Shiva decided that these bamboo harps were to form the basis of all music on Bali, because humans had thereby received the ability to pay their reverence to the gods and to please them in a new way . . . ." Berendt, Joachim-Ernst, *The World is Sound: Nada Brahma, Music and the Landscape of Consciousness* (Rochester: Destiny Books, 1983), 176.

250 Ibid, 5-6. According to scientific findings, women have a more developed sense of sound and men, a sense of sight.

251 Anne Klein informs us, "Just as sound emerges from silence and is an expression of it; just as thoughts emerge from primordial clarity and are a manifestation of it, so in the course of the ritual, visualizations

appear from empty space. These visualized images are understood as manifestations of the emptiness or primordial purity of the birthless matrix that is the mind's own essenceless essence." Anne C. Klein, *Meeting the Great Bliss Queen* (Boston: Beacon Press, 1995) 174. Also see 178-9.

252   Richard Stoney states that the Sun goddess of the mountain's name Shiwa is pronounced Sheeva. The Hindu or Dravidian god Shiva as Ardhanarishvara is both male and female.

253   Joanna Hubbs states there are many legends associated with the golden woman. She is linked with the Ugraian Jumala of the Urals who left gold offerings to her on a tree. An old hunter in 1967 informed treasure seekers that the golden matrioska had been long hidden for protection. The Vikings had also searched for a legendary golden matrioska (made of solid gold). Joanna Hubbs, *Mother Russia, The Feminine Myth in Russian Culture* (Bloomington, Indiana: Indiana University Press, 1988), xii.

254   The Slavs have a mythology based on Indo-European and Indo-Iranian beliefs. There are many similarities between Hindu and early Slavic world mythologies, e.g: practice of cremation and belief in reincarnation; karma, in which like produces like; Also, women played an important part in religious ceremonies.

255   For more on Baba Yaga, see *Women who Dance with Wolves* by Clarissa Pinkola Estes, 1992; and Phillippa Rappoport's, *Doll Folktales of the East Slavs: Invocation of Women from the Boundary of Space and Time*, Ph.D. Dissertation, University of Virginia, 1997.

256   Wayne Schlepp, "Cinderella in Tibet," *Asian Folklore Studies*, 61: no. 1 (2002): 123.

257   Audited course by Starhawk, "Creating Rituals," (Fall Semester, 1994), Holy Names College, Oakland, California.

258   *Valkyries*, similar to *vily*, are shapeshifting birdwomen, funerary priestesses turned into hawks. The Sanskrit word *vilasa* meant a heavenly nymph who took care of the dead. (Walker 1988, 280); The sun in the Rig-Veda is frequently compared to a hawk circling in the air. Buffie Johnson in *Lady of the Beasts* (San Francisco: Harper Collins, 1988), 8, states the bird was used for magical purposes. The beak, wings, and feathers were used in ceremony, costumes, masks and headdresses. A common practice was to consume the heart or eyes of the bird so that one could obtain its prophetic powers.

259   Abraham Maslow, *Religion, Values, and Peak Experiences* (New York: Viking, 1964), iii-iv.

260   Here Ghosh speculates the creation of the Buddhist Tara may have been an attempt to unsurp the powers of the Hindu Durga. Mallar Ghosh, *Development of Buddhist Iconography in Eastern India: A Study of Tara, Prajnas of Five Tathagatas and Bhrikuti* (New Delhi, India: Munshiram Manohartal Publishers Pvt. Ltd., 1980), 27.

261   It occurred to me after reading two books by Sandra Ingerman: *Welcome Home: Following your Soul's Journey Home* (New York: Harper, 1993), and Sandra Ingerman, *Soul Retrieval, Mending the Fragmented Self* (New York: Harper, 1991), soul loss may have occurred due to childhood abuse and a lack of meaningful rites of passages offered in Western culture for girls. For a study of the acculturation of girls in America, see *The Body Project, An Intimate History of American Girls* by Joan Jacobs Brumberg (New York: Random House, 1997). For a photographic illustrative work on the image of the American woman—Amanda Cruz, Elizabeth A.T. Smith, and Amelia Jones, *Cindy Sherman: Retrospective* (New York: Thames & Hudson, 2001).

262   There is still no word to define the non-denominational woman of wisdom in the West who is interested in spiritual development. Some call her "priestess," but this has Christian overlays.

[263] I moved to San Francisco in the late sixties so had the full experience of the counterculture's Dionysian days of beauty and play, what I considered a kind of paradise on earth.

[264] Lama Tsering Everest, *The Heart of Compassion* excerpt read by the author, Padma Publishing / Chagdud Gonpa Foundation, 1999. sound cassette.

[265] Sekmet is the Egyptian lion-headed goddess.

[266] For more information on 'samadhi' as ecstasy, Georg Feuerstein, *The Yoga Tradition* (Prescott, AZ: Hohm Press, 2001), 252-254.

[267] Anna Kavan, *Julia and the Bazooka* (New York: Alfred A. Knopf, 1975), 10-11.

[268] Quasha, George, *Ainu Dreams* (Barrytown, NY: Station Hill Press, 1999), 127.

[269] Ibid., 134-135.

[270] Adams, Doug and Diane Apostolos-Cappadona, eds. *Dance as Religious Studies* (New York: Crossroads, 1990), 115.

[271] See Monica Sjoo's *The Norse Goddess* (Cornwall, England: dor dama press), 2000.

[272] B. N. Goswamy, *Essence of Indian Art* (San Francisco: Asian Art Museum of San Francisco, 1986), 19-20.

[273] Ibid.

[274] Ibid., 21

[275] Ibid., 50.

[276] Ananda K. Coomaraswamy, *The Dance of Shiva: On Indian Art and Culture* (New York: The Noonday Press, 1957), 41.

[277] Ibid., 505.

[278] *Oxford English Dictionary* (New York: University Press, 2003), http://dictionary.oed.com.

[279] Pushpendra Kumar, Tar*a The Supreme Goddess* (Delhi, India: Bhharatiya Vidya Prakashan, 1992), 101.

[280] The Bengali green goddess known as *Syama* is still worshiped today. D.C. Sircar, ed. *The Sakti Cult and Tara* (Calcutta, India: Calcutta University Press, 1967), 130.

[281] Bokar Rinpoche. *Tara the Feminine Divine* (San Francisco: Clearpoint Press, 1999), 44.

[282] China Galland, *Longing for Darkness* (New York: Penguin Books, 1990), 175.

283 John Blofeld, *Boddhisattva of Compassion* (Shambala Publications, Boston, 1988), 59.

284 Ibid, 107.

285 David Kinsley. *The Ten Mahavidyas* (Berkeley: University of California Press, 1997), 92-3.

286 K.K. Dasgupta, "Iconography of Tara" in *The Sakti Cult and Tara*, ed, D.C. Sircar (Calcutta, India: Calcutta University Press, 1967), 126.

287 China Galland describes this form of Tara as a dark female God, "the other side of everything she knew about God." China Galland, *Longing for Darkness* (New York: Penguin Books, 1990), 341.

288 Indra Majupuria, *Nepalese Women* (Kathmandu: Craftsmen Press, Ltd., 1985), 22.

289 Frederique Apffel Marglin, *Wives of the God-King: The Rituals of the Devadasis of Puri* (Delhi: Oxford University Press, 1985, 316f.) quoting Ananda K. Coomaraswamy, *Yakshas: Essays in Water Cosmology* (Delhi: Oxford University Press 1993), 41.

290 Heinrich Zimmer, *Myths and Symbols in Indian Art and Civilization* (Princeton: Princeton University Press, 1974), 163-4.

291 Malcolm Goodwin, *Angels: An Endangered Species* (New York: Simon and Schuster, 1990), 11.

292 "Feitian (Flying Apsaras)," http://www.chinavista.com/experience/fei/feitian.html.

293 Carol Christ, *Odyssey with the Goddess* (New York: Continuum, 1995), 78.

294 Jean Shinoda Bolen, *Crossing to Avalon* (San Francisco: Harper 1995), 249.

295 Ibid., 261.

GLOSSARY

aniconic: Symbolic or suggestive rather than literally representational.

animism: The belief that natural objects such as rivers and rocks possess a soul or spirit.

anthropomorphic: Describes the attribution of human motivation, characteristics, or behavior to inanimate objects, animals, or natural phenomena.

archetype: The original model, form or pattern after which other similar things are patterned.

Authentic Movement: Developed by Mary Whitehouse in 1965, Authentic Movement is a method born from dance, Jungian studies and movement therapy. It is a self directed form where each person has the opportunity to move to spontaneous inner authentic responses while being witnessed. This method allows for the discovery of a path or bridge between the conscious and unconscious. Gradually the invisible becomes visible and the inaudible heard. The entire process illuminates inner workings by placing them within a mythic, imaginistic framework. Authentic Movement practice is known to evoke a profound sense of empathy to both the mover and the witness.

baba: Short for *babushka*, a Slavic term for grandmother. *Znakharkas*, village healers or medicine women are also known to be called *babushkas* by villagers. *Znakharka* was given a negative connotation during Soviet times.

Baba Yaga: In a number of East European myths, Baba Yaga is the shapeshifting cannibalistic crone or old nature spirit witch who lives in a hut on the edge of the forest. She is the goddess of wisdom and death (bringing death of the ego) and through death, rebirth. Called the Bone Mother, she lives in a hut that stands on chicken legs and is surrounded by skulls.

dakini: In Tibetan Buddhism a female "sky walker," a woman who flies, or female "sky-dancer," one who does not walk on the ground. The dakini or "skygoer," is a female wisdom being referred to as an embodiment of enlightened compassionate activity, a spirit in a female form (of both divine and human manifestations). Dakinis are women who engage in flights of spiritual insight, ecstasy. They are protectors and transmitters of tantric Buddhist teachings.

darsan: Seeing and being seen by the deity.

152

<u>Dharma</u>: In Buddhism, Dharma refers to the corpus of Buddhist teachings.

<u>dharmakaya</u>: The experience of the transcendence of form of the five senses and realization of true 'thusness.' It is the Buddha body in its self-nature, which is the same as the Dharma body, the eternal indestructible true principle, the Buddha's original body. Dharmakaya is realized through transcendental wisdom.

<u>ecstasy</u>: Mystic or prophetic trance. Divine trance is ever-present at the core of every sense experience, mind-state, emotion, and sensual pleasure cultivated and refined through metaphysical insight.

<u>embodiment</u>: To personify, make corporeal, to incarnate, to represent bodily form.

<u>entheogen</u>: Plant substances that, when ingested, offer one an experience of the divine. In the past entheogens were commonly called "hallucinogens" or "psychedelics." The term means "becoming divine within."

<u>ethnography</u>: An anthropological method of studying small groups of subjects in their own environments, with results documented in both descriptive and interpretive findings.

<u>folk dress</u>: Folk dress, also called peasant and ethnic dress, is the traditional dress worn by people in the countryside, outside the urban environment. It is often embellished with cultural symbols, patterns and forms.

<u>goddess</u>: 1) A female of supernatural powers or attributes believed in and worshiped by a people. 2) A female being believed to be the source of life and worshiped as the principal deity in various religions. 3) An image of a female supernatural being.

<u>hermeneutics</u>: Hermeneutics is the science and methodology of interpretation especially of scriptural text.

<u>heuristic</u>: Of, or constituting an educational method in which learning takes place through discoveries that result from investigations made by the researcher.

<u>holotropic</u>: This composite word means "oriented toward wholeness" or "moving in the direction of wholeness." It suggests that normally we identify with only a fraction of who we really are. In holotropic states, we are offered a gateway to enable us to transcend narrow boundaries of the body ego and reclaim our full identity.

Holotropic Breathwork: Holotropic Breathwork is a term coined by Stanislav and Christina Grof to describe a therapeutic method of inducing non-ordinary, holotropic states of consciousness through an intensive form of breathwork which provides access to the unconscious and superconscious psyche.

iconography: Illustration of a subject by pictures or other visual representations.

imaginal: Relating to imagination, images or imagery.

magic: 1) The art that purports to control or forecast natural events, effects, or forces by invoking the supernatural, 2) The practice of using charms, spells or rituals in attempt to produce supernatural effects or to control events in nature.

mantra: Mantra from the Sanskrit root man "to think," is a sacred sound or phrase (such as *Om, Ah, Hum*), imbued with symbolic significance and spiritual blessings, and has a transformative effect on the mind of the individual reciting it.

metaphor: A figure of speech used to describe an allegory.

matrika: A Sanskrit term that generally is interpreted to mean Mother, as in the Asta Matrikas (the eight mothers). It also has connections to sound.

mythologem: A mythological motif, such as the hidden treasure, the walled garden or the animal-man.

mythopoeic: This term refers to that which is productive of myth-making.

mystical: Inspiring a sense of mystery and wonder, of a nature or import that by virtue of its divinity surpasses understanding.

Nada Yoga: Nada Yoga works with the emotions through toning. Toning acts as a bridge between form and the formless. It's goal is to purify and magnetize, activate and balance the chakras. When practiced correctly, one is able to release and heal repressed emotions and become receptive to subtle vibrations. When working with emotions through the voice, each note is meant to correspond to a particular emotion. By using this technique, one is also able to find one's own natural voice, or note that resonates for them.

nirmanakaya: The "emanation body." This term is usually used to describe the physical form of a buddha.

orant: Raised arm position to invoke help; epiphany stance.

psyche: A modern term to replace "the unconscious." It is the directive principle in the human being which guides its growth from the moment of conception forward. The psyche sets the pattern of growth and works to sustain it, throughout one's life.

rusalki: Female water spirits found by water sources and in trees; shapeshifters.

samadhi: The ecstatic or unitive state in which the meditator becomes one with the object of meditation; a profound radiance; the one-pointed contemplation in meditative absorption.

sambogakaya: "The enjoyment body" of the buddha made of light.

synchronicity: The quality of being simultaneous, concurrence of acts, events, or developments in times, coincidence.

subaltern: Related to a subordinate status.

supernatural: Attributable to the action or presence of a ghost, spirit, or other invisible agent; divine as opposed to human, or spiritual as opposed to material.

vily: Female spirits who live in the woods, mountains, and clouds. They possess the ability to shapeshift into beautiful naked girls, swans, horses, falcons, or wolves; funerary priestesses.

zoomorphism: The attribution of animal characteristics or qualities to a god or gods; the use of animal forms in symbolism, literature, or graphic representation.

BIBLIOGRAPHY

Abram, David. *The Spell of the Sensuous*. New York: Vintage Books, 1996.

Adam, Doug and Diane Apostolos-Cappadona, eds. *Dance as Religious Studies*. New York: Crossroads, 1990.

Aizenstat, Stephen. "DreamTending: Befriending the Archetypal Imagination." Abstract for Association for the Study of Dreams (ASD) Conference Program, Oakland, California, Sept. 21- Oct. 5, 2003.

Alexandre, Chandra. "Through Vulture's Eye with Peacock's Tail." Ph.D. diss., California Institute of Integral Studies, 2001. Dissertation Abstracts International 62 (2001): 2259A. Accession no. AAT3016601

Allione, Tsultrim. *Women of Wisdom*. London: Arkana, 1984.

Almaas, Hammed Ali. *Essence with The Elixir of Enlightenment: The Diamond Approach to Inner Realization*. York Beach, ME: Samuel Weiser, 1998.

_____. *Spacecruiser Inquiry: True Guidance for the Inner Journey*. Boston: Shambala, 2002.

Andrews, Ted. *Animal-Speak: The Spiritual and Magical Powers of Creatures Great and Small*. St. Paul: Llewellyn Publications, 1995.

_____. *The Sacred Power in Your Name*. St. Paul: Llewellyn Publications, 1990.

Appelbaum, David. "Ways of Knowing." *Parabola* 22: no. 1, (Spring 1997): 4.

Association for the Study of Dreams (ASD), http://www.asdreams.org/ (accessed November 2, 2003).

Atkinson, Clarissa W., Constance H. Buchanan and Margaret R. Miles, eds. *Immaculate and Powerful, The Female in Sacred Image and Social Reality*. Boston: Beacon Press, 1985.

Badiner, Allan Hunt, and Alex Grey. *Zig Zag Zen: Buddhism and Psychedelics*. San Francisco: Chronicle Books, 2002.

Baldick, Julian. *Animal and Shaman*. New York: New York University Press, 2000.

Barasch, Marc Ian. *Healing Dreams: Exploring the Dreams That Can Transform Your Life*. New York: Penguin Putnam, 2000.

Barber, Elizabeth Wayland. "On the Origins of the *vily/ rusalki*." In *Varia on the Indo-European Past: Papers in Memory of Marija Gimbutas*, edited by Miriam Robbins Dexter and Edgar C. Polome, 6-47. Washington, DC: Institute of the Study of Man, 1997.

_____. *Prehistoric Textiles*. Princeton: Princeton University Press, 1991.

_____. "The Curious Tale of the Ultra-Long Sleeve." In *Folk Dress in Europe and Anatolia*, edited by Linda Welters, 111-134. New York: Berg, 1999.

_____. *The Mummies of Urumchi*. New York: W.W. Norton, 1999.

_____. *Women's Work: The First 20,000 Years Women, Cloth, and Society in Early Times*. New York: W.W. Norton, 1994.

Baring, Anne. "The Dream of the Water—A Quest for the Numinous." Lecture at Jupiter Group, Oxford, England, April 2000.

_____, and Jules Cashford. *Myth of the Goddess*. London: Arkana, 1993.

Barks, Coleman. *The Essential Rumi*. San Francisco: Harper, 1995.

Baumgartner, Louise Dianne. *Erotic Wisdom*. Master's thesis, California Institute of Integral Studies, 1998. Masters Abstracts International 37 (1999): 1726.

Berendt, Joachim-Ernst. *The World is Sound: Nada Brahma, Music and the Landscape of Consciousness*. Rochester: Destiny Books, 1991.

Bhattacharyya, Bhaskar. *The Path of The Mystic Lover: Baul Songs of Passion and Ecstasy*. Rochester: Destiny Books, 1993.

Bhattcharyya, Narendra Nath. *History of the Sakta Religion*. New Delhi: Munshiram Manoharial Publishers Pvt. 1973.

_____. *The Indian Mother Goddess*. 2d ed. New Delhi: Manohar Book Service, 1977.

Billington, Sandra and Miranda Green. *The Concept of the Goddess*. London:Routledge, 1996.

Birnbaum, Lucia. *Black Madonnas: Feminism, Religion, & Politics in Italy*. Boston: Northeastern University Press, 1993.

_____. *Dark Mother: African Origins and Godmothers*. Lincoln, NE: iUniverse, 2001.

_____. "Dark Wheat and Red Poppies." Unpublished essay. 2003.

Blofeld, John. *Mantras*. New York: E.P. Dutton, 1977.

Bobula, Ida. "The Symbol of the Magna Mater." *American Journal of Archaeology*." 62: 2 (1958): 221-222.

Bokar Rinpoche. *Tara the Feminine Divine*. San Francisco: Clearpoint Press, 1999.

Bolen, Jean Shinoda. *Crossing to Avalon*. San Francisco: Harper, 1994.

Borel, France. "The Decorated Body." *Parabola*. 19, no. 3 (Fall 1994): 75.

Bosnak, Robert. *A Little Course in Dreams: A Basic Handbook of Jungian Dreamwork*. Boston: Shambala, 1998.

Boucher, Francois. *20,000 Years of Fashion: The History of Costume and   Personal Adornment*. New York: Harry N. Abrams, 1967.

Boulet, Susan Seddon. *Shaman: The Paintings of Susan Seddon Boulet*. San Francisco: Pomegranate Artbooks, 1989.

Braud, William and Rosemarie Anderson. *Transpersonal Research Methods of the Social Sciences: Honoring Human Experience*. Thousand Oaks, CA: Sage Publications, 1998.

Bridgman, P.N. *Reflections of a Physicist*. New York: Philosophical Library, 1950.

Briffault, Robert. *The Mothers*. New York: Antheneum, 1977.

Brighenti, Francesco. *Sakti Cult in Orissa*. New Delhi: D.K. Printworld (P) Ltd., 2001.

Brumberg, Joan Jacobs. *The Body Project, An Intimate History of American Girls*. New York: Random House, 1997.

Brunel, Pierre, ed. *Companion to Literary Myths: Heroes and Archetypes*. London: Routledge, 1996.

Buber, Martin. *The Knowledge of Man*. New York: Harper & Row, 1950.

Bulkeley, Kelly. *Spiritual Dreaming: A Cross-cultural and Historical Journey*, New York: Paulist Press, 1995.

_____. *The Wilderness of Dreams: Exploring the Religious Meanings of Dreams in Modern Western Culture*. Albany, NY: SUNY Press, 1994.

_____ and Wendy Doniger. "*Why Study Dreams? A Religious Studies Perspective*." Dreaming 3 (1993): 69-73.

Cameron, Julia. *The Vein of Gold: The Journey to Your Creative Heart*. New York: Jeremy P. Tarcher, 1996.

Campbell, Joseph. *The Masks of God, Primitive Mythology*. New York: Viking Press, 1969.

_____. *Oriental Mythology*. New York: Penguin Books, 1985.

Campbell, June. *Traveller in Space*. New York: George Braziller, 1996.

Carter, Susan Gail. "Amaterasu-O-Mi-Kami, Past and Present: An Exploration of the Japanese Sun Goddess from a Western Feminist Perspective." Ph.D. diss., California Institute of Integral Studies, 2001. Dissertation Abstracts International 62/02 (2001): 803. Accession no. AAT3004465

_____."Mirrors of Many Moons: Reflections on the Use and Meaning of the Mirror throughout History." Masters thesis. Thesis. California Institute of   Integral Studies, 1997. Masters Abstracts International 39 (2001): 1997. Accession no. AAT1400748

Castaneda, Carlos. *The Art of Dreaming*. New York: Harper Collins, 1993.

Cavalli-Sforza, Luigi Luca, Paolo Menozzi, and Alberto Piazza. *The History and Geography of Human Genes*. Princeton: Princeton University Press, 1994.

_____. "Genetic Evidence Supporting Marija Gimbutas' Work on the Origins of Indo-European People." In *From the Realm of the Ancestors*. ed. Joan Marler. Manchester: Knowledge, Ideas & Trends, 1997.

Chamberlain, Laura, "Embodying the Goddess Durga: A Pilgrimage to the Mother Goddess of Paradox." Master's thesis, California Institute of Integral Studies, 2001. Masters Abstracts International 140 (2002): 919. Accession no. AAT1407335

Changchub, Gyalwa and Namkhai Nyingpo. *Lady of the Lotus-Born: The Life and Times of Yeshe Tsogyal*. Translated by Padmarkara Translation Group. Boston: Shambala, 1999.

Chevalier, Jean and Alain Gheerbrant. *Dictionary of Symbols*. London: Penguin Books, 1996.

Christ, Carol. *Odyssey with the Goddess*. New York: Continuum, 1995.

Circlot, J.E. *A Dictionary of Symbols*. Translated by Jack Sage, 2d ed., New York: Dorset Press, 1971.

Clements, Jennifer."Organic Inquiry: Research in Partnership with Spirit." Unpublished manuscript, 2002.

Clements, Jennifer, Dorothy Ettling, Dianne Jenett, and Lisa Shields."Organic Inquiry: If Research Were Sacred." Unpublished manuscript, 1999.

_____. "If Research Were Sacred—An Organic Methodology." http://www. serpentina.com/research-x.html. (accessed November 8, 2003).

Clottes, Jean and David Lewis-Williams. *The Shamans of Prehistory*. New York: Harry N. Abrams, 1998.

Coles, Robert. *The Spiritual Life of Children*. Boston: Houghton Mifflin, 1990.

Coomaraswamy, Ananda K. *The Dance of Shiva: On Indian Art and Culture*. New York: The Noonday Press, 1957.

_____. *Yaksas: Essays in Water Cosmology*. Delhi: Oxford University Press, 1993.

Cooper, J.C. *An Illustrated Encyclopaedia of Traditional Symbols*. London: Thames & Hudson, 1992.

Coxhead, David and Susan Hiller. *Dreams: Visions of the Night*. New York: Crossroad Publishing, 1976.

Cruz, Amanda, Elizabeth A. T. Smith, and Amelia Jones. *Cindy Sherman: Retrospective*. New York: Thames & Hudson, 2001.

Culpepper, Emily. "Philosophia in a New Key: The Revolt of the Symbols." Ph.D. diss., Harvard University 1983 quoted in Jane Caputi "On Psychic Activism: Feminist Mythmaking." In *The Feminist Companion to Mythology*, ed. Caroline Larrington, 425-440. London: Pandora Press, 1992.

Cunliffe, Barry, ed. *The Oxford Illustrated Prehistory of Europe*. New York: Oxford University Press, 1994.

d'Alviella, Count Goblet. *The Migration of Symbols*. New York: University Books, 1956.

Danielou, Alain. *Gods of Love and Ecstasy: The Traditions of Shiva and Dionysus*. Rochester, NY: Inner Traditions, 1992.

_____. *The Myths and Gods of India*. Rochester: Inner Traditions, 1985.

Dasgupta, K.K., "Iconography of Tara." *In The Sakti Cult and Tara*, ed. D.C. Sircar, 115–127. Calcutta: Calcutta University Press, 1967.

Daumel, Rene. *Rasa or Knowledge of the Self: Essays on Indian Aesthetics and Selected Sanskrit Studies*. Toronto, Canada: New Directions, 1983.

Davidson, H.R. Ellis. *Myths and Symbols in Pagan Europe*. Syracuse, NY: Syracuse University Press, 1988.

Davis-Kimball, Jeannine. *Warrior Women*, New York: Warner Books, 2002.

Day, Jeff. "Gods and Goddesses of the Balts," http://www.geocities.com/cas111jd/balts/balt_gods2.htm. (accessed November 1, 2003).

Day, Terence P. "The Twenty-One Taras: Features of a Goddess Pantheon in Mahayana Buddhism." In *Goddesses in Religions and Modern Debate*, ed. Larry W. Hurtado, University of Manitoba, 1990.

DeSalvo, Louise. *Writing as a Way of Healing: How Telling Our Stories Transforms our Lives*. Boston: Beacon Press, 1999.

Deslauriers, Daniel. "Dreamwork in the Light of Emotional and Spiritual Intelligence." *Advanced Development Journal* 9, (2000): 1–18.

Deveroux, Paul. *Places of Power*. London: Blandford, 1999.

_____. *Symbolic Landscapes*. Glastonbury, U.K.: Gothic Image Publications, 1992.

Dexter, Miriam Robbins. "The Frightful Goddess: Birds, Snakes and Witches." In *Varia on the Indo-European Past: Papers in Memory of Marija Gimbutas*, ed. Miriam Robbins Dexter and Edgar C. Polome, 124-154. Washington, DC: Institute of the Study of Man Inc., 1997.

_____. ed. *The Living Goddesses*. Berkeley, CA: University of California Press 1999.

_____. ed. *Whence the Goddess*. New York: Pergamon Press, 1990.

Dodson Gray, Elizabeth, ed. *Sacred Dimension of Women's Experience*. Wellesley, MA: Roundtable Press, 1989.

Doehner, Sven. "Sound Transformation in Dream–Work: Nourishing the Soul." Unpublished article. 2003.

Dorson, Richard, M., ed. *Folklore and Folklife*. Chicago: University of Chicago, 1972.

Dowman, Keith. *Sky Dancer*. London: Arkana, 1984.

Downing, Charles. *Russian Tales and Legends*. New York: Henry Z. Walck, 1964.

Dunduliene, Prane. "Ancient Lithuanian Mythology and Religion," http://www.litnet.lt/litinfo/religion.html. (accessed November 9, 2003).

Dundzila, Audrius Vilius."Maiden, Mother, Crone: Goddesses from Prehistory to European Mythology and Their Reemergence in German, Lithuanian, and Latvian Romantic Dramas." Ph.D. diss., University of Wisconsin, 1991. Dissertation Abstracts International 52 (1991): 1738, Accession no. AAT 9124664

_____."Rasa: The Summer Solstice," (1991), http://www.geocities.

com/Athens/Oracle/2810/rasa.html. (accessed November 1, 2003).

Durdin-Robertson, Lawrence. *The Year of the Goddess: A Perpetual Calender of Festivals*. Wellingborough, England: The Aquarian Press, 1990.

Eck, Diana L. *Darsan*. Chambersburg, PA: Anima Books, 1985.

Eliade, Mircea. *Images and Symbols, Studies in Religious Symbolism*. Translated by Philip Mairet. New York: Search Book, 1969.

_____. *Myths, Dreams and Mysteries*. Translated by Philip Mairet. New York: Harper & Bros., 1960.

_____. *Myth of the Eternal Return*. Translated by W.R. Trask. Princeton: Princeton University Press, 1972.

_____. *Rites and Symbols of Initiation*. Translated by W.R. Trask. New York: Harper & Row, 1958.

_____. *Shamanism: Archaic Techniques of Ecstasy*. Translated by W.R. Trask. Princeton: Princeton University Press, 1972.

English, Elizabeth. *Vajrayogini*. Boston: Wisdom Publications, 2002.

Evans, Ivor H., ed. *Brewer's Dictionary of Phrase and Fable*. Centenary Edition Rev. New York: Harper & Row, 1981.

Everest, Lama Tsering. *The Heart of Compassion*. Excerpt read by the author. Padma Publishing / Chagdud Gonpa Foundation, 1999. sound cassette.

Farhi, Donna. *The Breathing Book*. New York: Henry Holt, 1996.

Farrar, Janet and Stewart. "The Witches' Goddess," unpublished article, http://web.raex.com/~gbuckley/BOS/GG/Goddess.htm. (accessed November 3, 2003).

Faulk, Nancy Auer and Rita M. Gross. *Unspoken Worlds, Women's Religious Lives*. Belmont, CA: Wadsworth Publishing Company, 1989.

Feinstein, David and Stanley Krippner, Ph.D. *The Mythic Path: Discovering the Guiding Stories of Your Past—Creating a Vision for your Future*. New York: Jeremy P. Tarcher, 1997.

Ferguson, Diana. *The Magickal Year*. New York: Quality Paperback Book Club, 1988.

Ferrier, Marina."Living on the Edge: Personal Experiences as the New Dispensation in the Age of Aquarius," Ph.D. diss., Pacifica Graduate Institute, 1999. Dissertation Abstracts International 62 (2001): 1572. Accession no. AAT3008506

Feuerstein, Georg. *The Yoga Tradition*. Prescott, AZ: Hohm Press, 2001.

Fierz-David, Linda. *Women's Dionysian Initiation*. Dallas, TX: Spring Publications, Inc., 1988.

Fiorenza, Elisabeth Schussler. "In Search of Women's Heritage." In *Weaving the Visions*, edited by Judith Plaskow and Carol P. Christ, 29-38. San Francisco: Harper & Row, 1989.

Fox, Matthew and Rupert Sheldrake. *The Physics of Angels: Exploring the Realm Where Science and Spirit Meet*. San Francisco: Harper, 1996.

Frazer, J.G. *The Golden Bough*. New York: Macmillan, 1951.

Freud, Sigmund. *The Interpretation of Dreams*. New York: Avon Books, 1965.

Froud, Brian and Alan Lee, eds. *Faeries*. New York: Harry N. Abrams, 1978.

Gackenbach, Jayne I. "Women and Meditators as Gifted Lucid Dreamers." In *Dreamtime & Dreamwork*, edited by Stanley Krippner, 244-251. New York: Tarcher Putnam, 1990.

Gadon, Elinor W. *The Once and Future Goddess*. San Francisco: Harper, 1989.

Galland, China. *The Bond Between Women*. New York: Penguin Putnam, 1998.

_____. *Longing for Darkness*. New York: Penguin Books, 1990.

Gass, Robert. *Chanting: Discovering Spirit in Sound*. New York: Random House, 1999.

Gendlin, Eugene T. *Focusing*. New York: Everest House, 1978.

Ghosh, Mallar. *Development of Buddhist Iconography in Eastern India: A Study of Tara, Prajnas of Five Tathagatas and Bhrikuti*. New Delhi, India: Munshiram Manohartal Publishers Pvt. Ltd., 1980.

Giedion, S. *The Eternal Present: The Beginnings of Art*. New York: Bollingen Foundation, 1962.

Gimbutas, Marija. *The Balts*. London: Thames and Hudson Ltd., 1963.

_____. *The Civilization of the Goddess: The World of Old Europe*. San Francisco: Harper, 1991.

_____. The *Goddesses and Gods of Old Europe, Myths and Cult Images*. Berkeley, CA: University of California Press, 1982.

_____. *The Language of the Goddess*. San Francisco: Harper Collins, 1991.

_____. *The Living Goddesses*. Edited by Miriam Robbins Dexter. Berkeley: University of California Press, 1999.

Gimbutas, Marija. *The Slavs*, London: Thames and Hudson Ltd, 1971.

Gitlin-Emmer, Susan. *Lady of the Northern Light: A Feminist Guide to Runes*. Freedom, CA: The Crossing Press, 1993.

Glueck, Nelson. *Deities and Dolphins*. New York: Farrar, Straus, and Giroux, 1965.

Goleman, Daniel. *Emotional Intelligence*. New York: Bantam Books, 1995.

Goodman, Felicitas. *Where the Spirits Ride the Wind: Trance Journeys and Other Ecstatic Experiences*. Bloomington: Indiana University Press, 1990.

Goodwin, Malcolm. *Angels: An Endangered Species*. New York: Simon and Schuster, 1990.

Gore, Belinda. *Ecstatic Body Postures: An Alternate Reality Workbook*. Santa Fe, NM: Bear & Co., 1995.

Gostelow, Mary. *Embroidery of All Russia*. New York: Charles Scribner's Sons, 1977.

_____. *Embroidery, Traditional Designs, Techniques and Patterns from All Over the World*. New York: Arco Publishing, 1983.

Goswamy, B.N. *Essence of Indian Art*. San Francisco: Asian Art Museum of San Francisco, 1986.

Gottner-Abendroth, Heide. *The Dancing Goddess*. Boston: Beacon Press, 1982.

Grahn, Judy. *Blood, Bread, and Roses*. Boston: Beacon Press, 1993.

Grame, Tricia. "Life into Art; Art into Life: Transformative Effects of the Female Symbol on a Contemporary Woman Artist." Ph.D. diss., California Institute of Integral Studies, 2000. Dissertation Abstracts International 61 (2000): 3806. Acession no. AAT9992390

Graves, Robert. *The White Goddess*. New York: Noonday Press, 1975.

Groff, Stanislav. *Beyond the Brain*. Albany, NY: SUNY Press, 1985.

_____. *The Holotropic Mind*. New York: HarperCollins, 1992.

Groff, Stanislav. *Psychology of the Future: Lessons from Modern Consciousness Research*. Albany: SUNY Press, 2000.

_____ and Chistina Grof. *Spiritual Emergency: When Personal Transformation Becomes a Crisis*. Los Angeles, Jeremy P. Tarcher, 1989.

Gross, Rita M., ed. *Beyond Androcentrism, New Essays on Women and Religion*, Missoula, MT: Scholars Press, 1977.

Gross, Rita M. *Feminism and Religion*. Boston: Beacon Press, 1996.

Guenon, Rene. *Fundamental Symbols, The Universal Language of Sacred Science*. Cambridge, England: Qunita Essentia, 1995.

Gunning, Tom. "Sacredness," http://www.materdei.ie/logos/sacredness%20article.htm. (accessed November 1, 2003).

Gyatso, Geshe Kelsang. *Guide to Dakini Land*. London: Tharpa Publications, 1991.

Gyatso, Janet. "Down with the Demoness: Reflections on a Feminine Ground in Tibet." In *Feminine Ground*. Janice Willis, 33-51. Ithaca: Snow Lion, 1987.

_____. *Apparitions of the Self: The Secret Autobiographies of a Tibetan Visionary.* Princeton, NJ: Princeton University Press, 1998.

Halifax, Joan. *The Fruitful Darkness*. New York: HarperCollins, 1993.

_____. *Shaman: The Wounded Healer*. London: Thames and Hudson, 1982.

Halifax, Joan. *Shamanic Voices*. New York: E.P. Dutton, 1979.

Halpern, Steven and Louis Savary. *Sound Health*. San Francisco: Harper & Row, 1985.

Harding, M. Esther. *Woman's Mysteries, Ancient and Modern*. Boston: Shambala, 1971.

Harner, Michael. *The Way of the Shaman*. Toronto, Canada: Bantam Books, 1986.

Hartman, Abbess Zenkei Blanche. "A Natural Action." (2000), http://www.intrex.net/chzg/hartman3.htm (accessed November 2, 2003).

Heilbrun, Carolyn. *Writing a Woman's Life*. New York: Ballantine Books, 1988.

Heinberg, Richard. *Celebrate the Solstice: Honoring the Earth's Seasonal Rhythms through Festival and Ceremony*. London: Quest Books, 1993.

Hillman, James. *The Soul's Code: In Search of Character and Calling*. New York: Random House, 1996.

Hilton, Alison. *Russian Folk Art*. Bloomington, IN: Indiana University Press, 1995.

Hobson, J.A. *The Dreaming Brain*. New York: Basic Books, 1988.

Houston, Jean. *A Mythic Life: Learning to Live Our Greater Story*. New York: Harper Collins, 1996.

_____. *The Search for the Beloved*. Los Angeles: Jeremy P. Tarcher, 1987.

Hubbs, Joanna. Mother Russia, *The Feminine Myth in Russian Culture*. Bloomington, IN: Indiana University Press, 1988.

Huld, Marin E. "The Childhood of Heroes: An Essay in Indo-European Puberty Rites." In *Varia on the Indo-European Past: Papers in Memory of Marija Gimbutas*, ed. Miriam Robbins Dexter and Edgar C. Polome, 176-193. Washington, DC: Institute of the Study of Man Inc., 1997.

Humes, Cynthia Ann. "Glorifying the Great Goddess or Great Woman." In *Women and Goddess Traditions*, ed. Karen L. King, Minneapolis, MN: Fortress Press, 1997.

Hunt, H. T. *The Multiplicity of Dreams: A Cognitive Psychological Perspective*. New Haven, CT: Yale University Press, 1989.

Ingerman, Sandra. *Soul Retrieval: Mending the Fragmented Self*. New York: HarperCollins, 1991.

_____. *Welcome Home*, New York: HarperCollins, 1993.

Ingram, Catherine. *Passionate Presence*. New York: Gotham Books, 2003.

James, E.O. *The Cult of the Mother-Goddess*. New York: Barnes & Noble, 1994.

James, William. *The Varieties of Religious Experience*. New York: Mentor Books, 1958.

Jansen, Eva Rudy. *Singing Bowls*. Diever, Holland: Binkey Kok Publications, 1992.

Jayakar, Pupul. *The Earth Mother*. San Francisco: Harper & Row, 1990.

Jenett, Dianne, "Red Rice for Bhagavati/cooking for Kannaki: an Ethnographic Inquiry of the Pongala Ritual at the Attukal Temple, Kerala, India." Ph.D. diss., California Institute of Integral Studies, San Francisco, 1999. Dissertation Abstract International 39 (2001). Accession no. AT9961566

_____. and Judy Grahn. http://www.serpentina.com/research/organic-ifresearchsacred.html. (accessed November 3, 2003).

Jettmar, Karl. *Art of the Steppes*. New York: Crown Publishers, 1967.

Joans, Shirley Ann, ed. *Simply Living*. Novato, CA: New World Library, 1999.

Johnson, Buffie. *Lady of the Beasts*. San Francisco: Harper Collins, 1988.

Judith, Anodea. *Wheels of Life: A User's Guide to the Chakra System.* St. Paul, MN: Llewellyn Publications, 1987.

Jung, Carl. *Memories, Dreams, and Reflections.* New York: Random House, 1961.

_____. *Dreams.* Princeton: Princeton University Press, 1974.

Kalwett, Holger. *Dreamtime & Inner Space.* Boston: Shambala, 1988.

Kason, Yvonne, M.D. and Teri Degler. *A Farther Shore: How Near-Death and Other Extraordinary Experiences Can Change Ordinary Lives.* Toronto, Canada: HarperCollins Publishers, 1994.

Kavan, Anna. *Julia and the Bazooka.* New York: Alfred A. Knopf, 1975.

Kelly, Mary B. *Goddess Embroideries of Eastern Europe.* McClean, NY: StudioBooks, 1996.

Kerenyi, C. *Asklepios.* New York: Bollingen Foundation, 1959.

King, Karen L., ed. *Women and Goddess Traditions In Antiquity and Today.* Minneapolis, MN: Fortress Press, 1997.

Kinsley, David R. *The Goddesses' Mirror, Visions of the Divine from East and West.* Albany, NY: SUNY Press, 1989.

_____. *Hindu Goddesses.* London: University of California Press, 1988.

_____. *The Ten Mahavidyas.* Berkeley, CA: University of California Press, 1997.

Klein, Anne C. *Meeting the Great Bliss Queen.* Boston: Beacon Press, 1995.

Knab, Sophie Hodorowicz. *Polish Customs, Traditions & Folklore.* New York: Hippocrene Books, 2002.

Krippner, Stanley, ed. *Dreamtime & Dreamwork: Decoding the Language of the Night.* New York: J.P. Putnam's Sons, 1990.

Krippner, Stanley, Fariba Bogzaran, and Andre Percia De Carvalho. *Extraordinary Dreams and How to Work with Them.* Albany, NY: SUNY Press, 2002.

Kumar, Pushpendra. *Tara The Supreme Goddess*. Delhi, India: Bhharatiya Vidya Prakashan, 1992.

Kungurtsev, Igor and Olga Luchakova. "The Unknown Russian Mysticism: Pagan Sorcery, Christian Yoga, and Other Esoteric Practices in the Former Soviet Union." *Gnosis* 31 (1994): 20-27.

La Barre, Weston. *The Ghost Dance*. New York: Dell, 1972

La Berge, Stephen and Howard Rheingold. *Exploring the World of Lucid Dreaming*. New York: Ballantine Books, 1990.

_____. *Lucid Dreaming: The Power of Being Awake & Aware in Your Dreams*. New York: Ballantine Books, 1985.

Lakoff, George and Mark Johnson. *Metaphors We Live By*. Chicago: University of Chicago Press, 1980.

Larrington, Carolyne, ed. *The Feminist Companion to Mythology*. London: Harper Collins, 1992.

Laski, Marghanita. *Ecstasy in Secular and Religious Experiences*. Los Angeles, Jeremy P. Tarcher, 1961.

Lauter, Estella. *Women as Mythmakers*. Bloomington: Indiana University Press, 1984.

Lawlor, Robert. *Voices of the First Day*. Rochester, NY: Inner Traditions, 1991.

Lerner, Gerda. *Why History Matters*. New York: Oxford University Press, 1997.

Lewis, I.M. *Ecstatic Religion*. Harmondsworth: Penguin Books, 1971.

Lings, Martin. *Symbol & Archetype: A Study of the Meaning of Existence*, Cambridge, U.K.: Qunita Essentia, 1991.

Lipsey, Roger. *An Art of Our Own*. Boston: Shambala, 1988.

Lippard, Lucy R. *From the Center*. New York: E.P. Dutton, 1976.

_____. *Overlay, Contemporary Art and the Art of Prehistory*. New York: New Press, 1983.

Liungman, Carl G. *Dictionary of Symbols*. Santa Barbara, CA: ABC-CLIO, 1991.

Lonsdale, Steven. *Animals and the Origins of Dance*. New York: Thames and Hudson, 1981.

Lorde, Audre. *Sister Outsider*. Freedom, CA: The Crossing Press, 1984.

Majupuria, Indra. *Nepalese Women*. Kathmandu, Nepal: Craftsmen Press, Ltd., 1985.

Mamonova, Tatyana. *Women and Russia*. Boston: Beacon Press, 1984.

Mander, Anica Vesel. *Blood Ties*. New York: Random House, 1976.

_____. *Feminism as Therapy*. New York: Random House, 1974.

Marable, Virginia Marie. *Cross-Cultural Symbolism of Color*, Ph.D. diss., United States International University, 1991. Dissertation Abstracts International 52 (1991): 981. Accession no. AAT3026601

Marglin, Frederique Apffel. *Wives of the God-King: The Rituals of the Devadasis of Puri*. Delhi, India: Oxford University Press, 1985.

Marler, Joan, ed. *From the Realm of the Ancestors, An Anthology in Honor of Marija Gimbutas*. Manchester: Knowledge, Ideas and Trends, 1997.

Marshack, Alexander. *The Roots of Civilization*. New York: McGraw Hill, 1972.

Marshall, Peter. *Nature's Web*. New York: Paragon House, 1994.

Maslow, Abraham. *Religion, Values, and Peak Experiences*. New York: Viking, 1964.

Matthews, Boris, trans. *The Herder Symbol Dictionary, Symbols from Art, Archaeology, Mythology, Literature, and Religion*. Wilmette, IL: Chiron Publications, 1986.

Matthews, Caitlin and John Matthews. *The Western Way, A Practical Guide to the Western Mystery Tradition*. London: Arkana, 1985.

McCrickard, Janet. *Eclipse of the Sun, An Investigation into Sun and Moon Myths*. Glastonbury, U.K.: Gothic Image Publications, 1990.

McLean, Adam. *The Triple Goddess: An Exploration of the Archetypal Feminine*. Grand Rapids, MI: Phanes Press, 1989.

Meehan, Aidan. *The Tree of Life*. New York: Thames and Hudson, 1995.

Meier, Carl Alfred. *Healing Dream and Ritual*. Einsiedeln: Daimon Verlag, 1989.

Meloy, Judith M. *Writing the Qualitative Dissertation: Understanding by Doing*. Mahwah, NJ: Lawrence Erlbaum Assoc., 2002.

Mellart, James. Catal Huyuk: *A Neolithic Town in Anatolia*. New York: McGraw-Hill, 1972.

Metzger, Deena. *Writing for Your Life: A Guide and Companion to the Inner Worlds*. San Francisco: Harper, 1992.

Metzner, Ralph. *Green Psychology: Transforming Our Relationship to the Earth*. Rochester, NY: Park Street Press, 1999.

_____. *Well of Remembrance, Rediscovering the Earth Wisdom Myths of Northern Europe*. Boston: Shambala, 1984.

_____. *The Unfolding Self: Varieties of Transformative Experience*. Novato: Origin Press, 1998.

Migne, J.P., ed. *Hildegard of Bingen, Patrologia Latina*. Paris: Migne, 1844-1891.

Minyonok Sergei and Yelena Minyonok. "Video Encyclopedia of Russian Folklore," In *SEEFA Journal*, 2: no.2 (Fall 1997): 26-31.

Mladenovic, Vesna. "Threads of Life: Red Fringes in Macedonian Dress," In *Folk Dress in Europe and Anatolia*. ed. Linda Welters, 97-110. New York: Berg, 1999.

Moon, Beverly, ed. *An Encyclopedia of Archetypal Symbolism*. Boston: Shambala, 1991.

Morton, Nelle. "The Goddess as Metaphoric Image." In *Weaving the Visions*, ed. Judith Plaskow and Carol P. Christ, 111-118. San Francisco: Harper&Row,1989.

Moustakas, Clark. *Heuristic Research*. Newbury Park, CA: Sage, 1990.

Muktananda, Swami. *Nothing Exists That Is Not Shiva*. South Fallsburg, NY: Siddha Yoga Publications, 1997.

Mullen, Glenn. *Female Buddhas*. Santa Fe, NM: Clearlight Publishers, 2003.

Muller-Ebeling, Claudia, Christian Ratsch, and Surendra Bahadur Shahi. *Shamanism and Tantra in the Himalayas*. Rochester, NY: Inner Traditions, 2000.

Murrell, Beatrix, "Noetic Gnosis: Cosmic Consciousness," http://www. csp.org/experience/docs/noetic_gnosis.html (accessed November 8, 2003).

Nakkach, Silvia. "Sacred Sound, the Creator and the Transformer," http://www.voxmundiproject.com/sacredsound.html (accessed November 8, 2003).

Neumann, Erich. *The Great Mother*. Princeton: Princeton University Press, 1963.

Nicholson, Shirley, ed. *The Goddess Re-Awakening*, The Feminine Principle Today. Wheaton, IL: Theosophical Publishing House, 1989.

Noble, Vicki. *Double Goddess*. Rochester, NY: Bear & Co., 2003.

_____. *Shakti Woman, Feeling our Fire, Healing our World*. San Francisco: Harper, 1991.

_____, ed. *Uncoiling the Snake, Ancient Patterns in Contemporary Women's Lives*. San Francisco: Harper, 1993.

Namkhai Norbu. *Dream Yoga and the Practice of Natural Light*. Edited by Michael Katz. Ithaca, NY: Snow Lion, 1992.

O'Flaherty, Wendy Doniger. *Dreams, Illusion and Other Realities*. Chicago: University of Chicago Press, 1984.

Oleszkiewicz, Malgorzata. "Mother of God and Mother Earth: Religion, Gender and Transformation in East-Central Europe." Unpublished article, n.d.

Olson, Carl, ed. *The Book of the Goddess Past and Present*. New York: Crossroads, 1986.

Orenstein, Gloria Fenman. *The Reflowering of the Goddess*. New York: Pergamon Press, 1990.

Otto, Rudolph. *The Idea of the Holy*. 2d ed. Translated by John W. Harvey. Oxford, England: Oxford University Press, 1950.

Oxford English Dictionary (Online) (OED). New York: University Press, 2002. http://dictionary.oed.com. (accessed November 1, 2003).

Paine, Sheila. *Afghan Amulet*. New York: St. Martin's Press, 1994.

_____. *Embroidered Textiles, Traditional Patterns from Five Continents*. London: Thames and Hudson, 1990.

Pinkola Estes, Clarissa. *Women Who Run with the Wolves: Myths and Stories of the Wild Woman Archetype*. New York: Ballantine Books, 1992.

Polanyi, Michael. *The Tacit Dimension*. Garden City, NY: Doubleday, 1966.

Polome, Edgar, C. "Animals in IE Cult and Religion." In *Varia on the Indo-European Past: Papers in Memory of Marija Gimbutas*. edited by Miriam Robbins Dexter and Edgar C. Polome, 6-47. Washington, DC: Institute of the Study of Man Inc., 1997.

Powell, James N. *The Tao of Symbols, How to Transcend the Limits of Our Symbolism*. New York: Quill, 1982.

Progoff, Ira. *The Symbolic & the Real*. New York: McGraw-Hill Book, 1963.

_____. *The Well and the Cathedral*. New York: Dialogue House Library, 1977.

Purkiss, Diane. "Women's Rewriting of Myth." In *The Feminist Companion to Mythology*, ed. Carolyne Larrington, London: Pandora Press, 1992.

Quasha, George. *Ainu Dreams*. Barrytown, NY: Station Hill Press, 1999.

Radha, Swami Sivananda. *Kundalini Yoga for the West*. Boston: Shambala, 1985.

_____. *Realities of the Dreaming Mind*, WA. Spokane: Timeless Books, 1994.

Rappoport, Philippa. "Doll Folktales of the East Slavs: Invocation of Women from the Boundary of Space and Time." Ph.D. diss., University of Virginia, 1997. Dissertation Abstracts International 59 (1998): 509. Accession no. AAT9824292

Raudvere, Catharina. "Now You See Her, Now You Don't: Some Notes on the Conception of Female Shape-Shifters in Scandinavian Traditions." In *The Concept of the Goddess*, ed. Sandra Billington and Miranda Green, 41-55. London: Routledge, 1996.

Reynolds, John Myrdhin. "The Wrathful Lion-Headed Dakini" http://www.angelfire.com/vt/vajranatha/simha.html. (accessed November 3, 2003).

Rickard, Allyson. *Tara Practice: Cultivating the Chi of the Black Sect Tantric Buddhist Feng Shui Practitioner*. Unpublished manuscript, 2001.

Rico, Gabriele, Lusser. *Writing the Natural Way: Using Right-Brain Techniques to Release Your Expressive Powers*. Los Angeles: J.P. Tarcher, 1983.

Ricoeur, Paul. *The Conflict of Interpretations*. Evanston, IL: Northwestern University Press, 1974.

Rogers, Carl. *Client-centered Therapy*. Boston: Houghton-Mifflin, 1951.

Sablatura, Patricia Ann. "The Experience of the Numinous in the Imaginal Dream Group Process known as Dreamtending." Ph.D. diss., Pacifica Graduate Institute, 2001. Dissertation Abstracts International 62 (2001): 2500. Accession no. AAT3015789

Saliklis, Ruta. *The Dynamic Relationship Between Lithuanian National Costumes and Folk Dress In Folk Dress in Europe and Anatolia*, ed. Linda Welters, 211-234. New York: Berg, 1999.

Sardello, Robert, ed. *The Angels*. New York: Continuum, 1995.

Schlepp, Wayne. "Cinderella in Tibet." *Asian Folklore Studies* 61: no.1 (2002): 123-148.

Schneider, Michael. *A Beginner's Guide to Constructing the Universe*. New York: Harper, 1994.

Schrei, Robert. "The Plant Medicine Sutra." In *Zig Zag Zen: Buddhism and Psychedelics*, ed. Allan Hunt Badiner and Alex Grey, 23. San Francisco: Chronicle Books, 2002.

Schultes, Richard Evans and Albert Hoffman. *Plants of the Gods: Origins of Hallucinogenic Use*. New York: Alfred van der Marck Editions, 1987.

Schuster, Carl and Edmund Carpenter. *Patterns That Connect, Social Symbolism in Ancient and Tribal Art*. New York: Harry N. Abrams, Inc., 1996.

Scully, Vincent. *The Earth, The Temple, and the Gods*. New Haven, CT: Yale University Press, 1962.

Sellers Susan, ed. *The Helene Cixous Reader*. London: Routledge, 1994.

Sharma, Arvind and Katherine K. Young, eds. *Feminism and World Religions*. Albany, NY: SUNY Press, 1999.

_____. *Today's Woman in World Religions*. Albany, NY: State University of New York Press, 1994.

_____. *Women in World Religions*. Albany, NY: State University of New York Press, 1987.

Shaw, Miranda. "Delight in this World." *Parabola*. 23: no. 2 (Summer, 1998): 39.

_____. *Passionate Enlightenment*. Princeton: Princeton University Press, 1994.

Shearer, Cindy. "Making Sense: Writing as Means of Defining Cultural Life." Unpublished article. 1996.

Sigrist, Robert. "Apophatic Mysticism: The Capture of Happiness." http://www.apophaticmysticism.com/definitions.html. (accessed November 8, 2003).

Simmer-Brown, Judith. *Dakini's Warm Breath*. Boston: Shambala, 2001.

Sinetar, Marsha. *Ordinary People as Monks and Mystics: Lifestyles for Self-Discovery*. New York: Paulist Press, 1973.

Singers of the Art of Living. *Sacred Chants of Shiva: From the Banks of the Ganges*. Produced by Craig Pruess. www.sonarupa.co.uk/itm00674.htm (accessed November 8, 2003).

Sircar, D.C., ed. *The Sakti Cult and Tara*, Calcutta: Calcutta University Press, 1967.

Skafte, Dianne. *Listening to the Oracle: Understanding the Signs & Symbols All Around Us*. New York: HarperSanFrancisco, 1997.

Sjoo, Monica. *The Norse Goddess*. Cornwall: dor dama press, 2000.

Smith, Huston. *Why Religion Matters*. New York: HarperCollins Publishers, 2001.

Smithers, Stuart. "Bodies of Sleep, Garments of Skins." *Parabola*. 9: no. 3 (1994): 7.

Spretnak, Charlene. *States of Grace*. New York: Harper San Francisco, 1991.

Stuckey, Marc. "A Heuristic Investigation of Presence," Ph.D. diss., California Institute of Integral Studies, 2001. Dissertation Abstracts International 62 (2001): 2965. Accession no. AAT3016608

Sullivan, Kathleen. *Recurring Dreams: A Journey to Wholeness*. Freedom, CA: Crossing Press, 1998.

Swan, James A. *Sacred Places*. Santa Fe, NM: Bear & Company, 1990.

Tart, Charles. *Altered States of Consciousness*. New York: John Wiley & Sons, 1969.

_____."World simulation in waking and dreaming." *Journal of Mental Imagery* 11 (1987): 145-158.

Taylor, Jeremy. *Where People Fly and Water Runs Uphill*. New York: Warner Books, 1992.

Temple, Robert. *The Genius of China: 3,000 Years of Science, Discovery and Invention*. New York: Simon & Schuster, 1986.

Tenzin Wangyal Rinpoche. *Healing with Form, Energy and Light: The Five Elements in Tibetan Shamanism, Tantra, and Dzogchen*. Ithaca, NY: Snow Lion, 2002.

_____. *The Tibetan Yogas of Dream and Sleep*. Ithaca, NY: Snow Lion, 1998.

_____. *Wonders of the Natural Mind: The Essence of Dzogchen in the Native Bon Tradition of Tibet*. Ithaca, NY: Snow Lion, 2000.

Thurman, Robert. *Circling the Sacred Mountain*. New York: Bantam Books, 1999.

_____. *Inner Revolution*. New York: Riverhead Books, 1998.

Torjesen, Karen Jo. *When Women Were Priests*. San Francisco: Harper, 1995.

Tulku, Tarthang. *Openness Mind*. Berkeley, CA: Dharma Press, 1978.

Vilenskaya, Larissa. "From Slavic Mysteries to Contemporary Psi Research and Back," Part 1, 2 and 3. Unpublished articles, n.d.

Volpe, Angela Della. "The Great Goddess, the Sirens and Parthenope." In *Varia on the Indo-European Past: Papers in Memory of Marija Gimbutas* ed. Miriam Robbins Dexter and Edgar C. Polome, 83-123 Washington DC: Institute of the Study of Man, Inc., 1997.

Walker, Barbara, G. *The Secrets of the Tarot*. San Francisco: Harper Collins, 1984.

_____. *The Women's Dictionary of Symbols and Sacred Objects*. San Francisco: Harper Collins, 1988.

_____. *The Women's Encyclopedia of Myths and Secrets*. Edison, NJ: Castle Books, 1996.

Warner, Marina. *Alone of All Her Sex, The Myth and The Cult of the Virgin Mary*. New York: Vintage Books, 1983.

Washburn, Michael. *The Ego and the Dynamic Ground*. Boston: Shambala, 1988.

Watkins, Mary. *Invisible Guests: The Development of Imaginal Dialogues*. Hillsdale, NJ: Lawrence Erlbaum Associates, Inc., 1986.

_____. *Waking Dreams*. Dallas, TX: Spring Publications, 1992.

Watts, Alan. *The Way of Zen*. Toronto, Canada: Vintage Books, 1957.

Welters, Linda. "Introductions: Folk Dress, Supernatural Beliefs, and the Body." In *Folk Dress in Europe and Anatolia*, ed. Linda Welters, 1-12, New York: Berg, 1999.

White, Rhea, "Becoming More Human as We Work: The Reflexive Role of Exceptional Human Experience.' In William Braud and Rosemarie Anderson, *Transpersonal Research Methods of the Social Sciences*: Honoring Human Experience. Thousand Oaks: Sage Publications, 1998, 128-45.

White, Rhea. http://www.ehe.org/display/ehe-menu.cfm?sectid=14. (accessed November 2, 2003).

Wickpedia. "Slavic Peoples." http://www.wikipedia.org/wiki/Slavic_people (accessed November 9, 2003).

Wilber, Ken. *No Boundary*. Boston: Shambala, 1979.

Willson, Martin. *In Praise of Tara*. Boston: Wisdom Publications, 1996.

Williams, C.A.S. *Outlines of Chinese Symbolism & Art Motives*. New York: Dover Publications, Inc., 1976.

Williams, Sharon. "A Path into the Forest." Ph.D. diss., California Institute of Integral Studies, 2002. Dissertation Abstracts International 63 (2002): 622. Accession no. AAT3042881

Willis, Janice D. "Dakini: Some Comments on its Nature and Meaning." In *Feminine Ground*, ed. Janice Willis. Ithaca, NY: Snow Lion, 1987.

Wolf, Fred Alan. *The Dreaming Universe: A Mind-Expanding Journey into the Realm where Psyche and Physics Meet*. New York: Simon & Schuster, 1994.

Womack, Yana. "Women, *Sakti*, and the Goddess: An Investigation on the Veneration of Hindu Female Deities," unpublished Master's thesis. New College of California, 1999.

Yogi Hari. "Nada Yoga - The Yoga of Sound." http://www.yogihari.com/nada-yoga.htm (accessed November 3, 2003).

Young, Serinity. *Dreaming the Lotus: Buddhist Dream Narrative, Imagery, and Practice*. Somerville, MA: Wisdom Publications, 1999.

Zimmer, Heinrich. *Myths and Symbols in Indian Art and Civilization*. Princeton, NJ: Princeton University Press, 1974.

Ziolkowski, Mari P. "Fierce Shakti/Fierce Love: A Feminist, Heuristic, Transpersonal Encounter with the Hindu Goddess Kali Ma." Ph.D. diss., California Institute of Integral Studies, 2003. Dissertation Abstracts International 64 (2003): 309. Accession no. AAT3078806

Zukov, Gary. *The Seat of the Soul*. New York: Simon & Schuster, 1990.

I want morebooks!

Buy your books fast and straightforward online - at one of the world's
fastest growing online book stores! Environmentally sound due to
Print-on-Demand technologies.

Buy your books online at
www.get-morebooks.com

Kaufen Sie Ihre Bücher schnell und unkompliziert online – auf einer der am
schnellsten wachsenden Buchhandelsplattformen weltweit!
Dank Print-On-Demand umwelt- und ressourcenschonend produziert.

Bücher schneller online kaufen
www.morebooks.de

SIA OmniScriptum Publishing
Brivibas gatve 1 97
LV-103 9 Riga, Latvia
Telefax: +371 68620455

info@omniscriptum.com
www.omniscriptum.com

Printed in Great Britain
by Amazon

84935123R00112